BASIC
yoga

BASIC
yoga

Susannah Marriott

BARNES
&NOBLE
BOOKS
NEW YORK

Acknowledgments

Thanks as ever to my yoga teachers, Rima and Nita Patel, especially to Rima for allowing me to teach her class. Thanks also to Marilyn Barnett for all the insight gained while editing her book Hot Yoga. I would like to thank everyone at MQP, especially Abi, Hilary, and, of course, Ljiljana.

Caution

If you are pregnant, have given birth in the last six weeks, or have a medical condition, such as high blood pressure, spinal problems, arthritis, or asthma, consult your medical practitioner or an experienced teacher before any exercise.

This edition published by Barnes & Noble, Inc. by arrangement with MQ Publications Limited

2004 Barnes & Noble Books

M 10 9 8 7 6 5 4 3 2 1
ISBN 0-7607-5297-4

Design: Balley Design Associates
Photography: Stuart Boreham

Printed in China

contents

foreword

Today, people want more from an exercise experience than simply to feel the burn. A workout increasingly has to have a special and personal appeal to distinguish it from the huge menu of options out there. Often, what people are looking for is something that inspires the mind and spirit while they work on the body, which might explain the explosion of aerobics classes with a music element—punk rock, gospel, street R&B, and so on. We also expect more of our leisure time these days; many of us want to feel our spirits lifted and to be transported far from the everyday world.

For thousands of years and across the continents, yoga has met this need. Yoga hones the body, building muscles, flexibility, and stamina. At the same time, it offers the mind complete relaxation, bringing about inner peace, and endowing you with new reservoirs of energy to draw on. Unlike many forms of exercise, this combination of body power and mind relaxation leaves you tingling all over, like a spiritual fix.

I was introduced to yoga at school, but let my practice lapse for many years, instead trying out every new fitness craze—aerobics, military-style circuit training, step, salsacise, aquacise, even deep-water aquacise. Only kickboxing brought me the mind-body union I was unknowingly craving.

When I became pregnant and had to give up kickboxing (the teacher had to kick me out of class) I came back to yoga but was frustrated at the slowness and lack of movement. Then I went to India to work on a yoga book with guru of hatha yoga, BKS Iyengar. The mist cleared. Inspired by the people I met, I returned to yoga, and found it gave me the flutters inside and a feeling that everything was as it should be, something I'd previously only got from listening to John Coltrane, from standing next to the speakers at reggae dances, from dancing in clubs to jazz. It brought me fleeting glimpses of something very special—call it inspiration, creativity, a sense of complete-ness—transcendence even. I hope this introduction to yoga brings you not just the body-defining and mind-calming experience you desire, but this extra something, too.

Susannah Marriott

introduction

- body benefits
- mind benefits
- getting started
- how to use this book

body benefits

Lengthened muscles, boosted strength and endurance, increased range of movements, well-aligned posture: yoga helps you tick this vital checklist to ward off the physical signs of ageing and keep you looking and feeling your very best.

realigning your posture

None of us has perfect posture: injuries and long-established negative patterns of movement pull us out of alignment and can lead to pain and further injury. Yoga encourages the spine and muscles to return to their ideal state, reshaping the body by restoring the full range of movement to areas damaged by injury and warped by bad habits. This has a positive impact on your every action, and so can transform your life.

Backache affects four out of five people at some stage in life. Yoga postures work, above all, to restore the natural curves to the spine, permit adequate blood flow and bring space around the vertebrae. This alignment helps to regulate and rebalance the flow of energy around the body: yoga theory holds that the most important, invisible, energy channel runs alongside the spine, governing the flow of life-force to every part of the body, and building a calm, focused, and connected state of mind.

below > **Standing poses boost strength and endurance while increasing flexibility.**

improving strength and flexibility

Everyone knows that yoga makes you more flexible, but were you aware that it builds strength, too? Muscles work in pairs, one stretching as its opposite shortens. In a yoga pose, therefore, you experience a lengthening as one muscle extends, and a simultaneous strengthening as the opposing muscle contracts. In this way, your body learns to balance strength and power with flexibility and fluidity. You don't use weights to work out in yoga, but as you work through the poses, you are constantly shifting and bearing your own body weight. Weight-bearing exercise helps prevent osteoporosis later in life. In addition, when your muscles have good tone, every part of your body works well: your standing and sitting posture improves, movement becomes easier, and you access a new store of energy, since each of your actions will require less effort.

building stamina

Some yoga postures can be surprisingly energetic, working the heart and lungs even though the body remains still. Your physical endurance builds as you perfect the postures, and your capacity to take in more oxygen develops as your chest and lungs expand, boosting the body's ability to deliver oxygen to muscles that require it. Many yoga postures act to slow the heart rate, while work on your breathing deepens and lengthens the flow of breath in and out. Yoga theory contends that this extends your lifespan.

promoting healthy joints

Joints are the parts of the body where the bones meet, and having flexibility in the joints, together with the stability that comes when the body is perfectly aligned, enables you to

above> **Stretching the spine makes you feel vital and energized.**

experience a full range of movement. With age and misuse or lack of use, joints lose their range of movement; yoga helps prevent this. Many yoga poses pay particular attention to enabling movement in the major joints of the body—the shoulders, hips, knees, and ankles—which, when aligned, allow your weight to be distributed evenly down into the floor. This helps ensure perfect posture.

cleansing from the inside

As you boost the circulation of your blood around the body by moving through the sequences of postures, oxygen and nutrients are taken effortlessly to every site that needs them. Equally, waste products are carried away—in sweat, with each exhalation, and as a result of stimulating the flow of lymph, the body's waste-disposal system. Specific poses massage the internal organs and vital glands, by exerting pressure on them from other parts of the body—the front of the thighs pressing on the abdomen, for example. This pressure and release is thought to promote good functioning and the elimination of toxins.

mind benefits

Many people come to yoga because they want to learn to switch off and relieve mental stress, but when you first start practicing, it can be difficult to tune in. Thoughts assault you from every direction and the mind chatters on unceasingly, preventing you from releasing the stress and relaxing completely.

relaxing the mind

After you have practiced yoga for a while, you focus on where your limbs are in a pose and on synchronizing your breath with the movement. As a result, you find you have effortlessly stopped the chatter of intruding thoughts and are able to relax completely. And as you let go of tightness in your body, you can release the thoughts and worries that cause tension and restriction in the mind.

deepening the breath

Pranayama is Sanskrit for yoga breathing techniques. It means "control" or "restraint" *(yama)* of the breath or life-force *(prana)*. In many of the breath-control techniques taught in yoga, you work consciously to lengthen and deepen the breath, which slows the heart rate, allows adequate oxygen to nourish every body system, and restores mental and emotional equanimity. Yoga is a unique exercise system because it co-ordinates the flow of breath in and out of your lungs with the movement of your limbs. When you bring your attention to your breathing in a pose, you fix yourself in the present—all worries about past actions or anticipation of future activities are wiped out and you exist in the moment, meditating in motion. Hence one of the earliest definitions of yoga—the cessation of the fluctuations of the mind. When you achieve this, even if only fleetingly, you experience an unforgettable sense of equilibrium and connection that is peace of mind.

energizing

In active yoga poses you work with your breath, harnessing the power of oxygen and the life-force to invigorate every cell. Other poses work to awaken the creative and nurturing spiritual energy known as *kundalini* that lies dormant deep within each of us. At the end of each yoga session, you settle into a posture known as Corpse Pose in which you remain motionless and without thoughts, your muscles completely relaxed and your mind in neutral. This is perhaps the most difficult yoga posture, since it involves switching the mind into meditative mode, but it is also the most rejuvenative and energizing. When you are completely relaxed, your body and mind are able to recharge and you emerge revitalized and ready to engage effectively with the world again.

getting to know yourself

As you practice yoga poses over weeks and months, you get to learn more about yourself: not only about how flexible your limbs and spine are, but where patterns of tension sit in your body, and how they alter within each posture. You begin to understand how your mind shrinks away from difficult tests, and watch how it becomes anxious to move on to new challenges even when your body isn't ready. You learn to recognize your response to the world, to difficulties and stress, and to discern how to make tiny changes that take you nearer to how you want to be. The

practice of yoga postures thus brings you an awareness of who you are and how you want to change. Above all, you get to realize that everything changes all the time; you are not at the stage you were at last week or last month: you are constantly developing. This knowledge can be very empowering and reassuring.

the power of patience

Be gentle with yourself when you practice yoga, letting go of expectations about getting what you want immediately. Don't expect to

above > **Meditation is an easy and enjoyable way to relax, either before the day starts or at the end.**

achieve the final pose effortlessly. Foresee your yoga practice rolling out gradually, and make yourself a vow to stay with it for months or years, rather than a few weeks. Chart your progress month by month rather than day by day. If you fine-tune a posture over days and weeks, you'll astound yourself with your progress when you stand back to assess where you are every couple of months.

getting started

Begin slowly, practice regularly, and enjoy the gradual changes for the better that you will feel in both body and mind.

what to wear

Loose, comfortable clothing is best; avoid anything that restricts your abdomen or throat. Always work barefoot, which allows you to grip the floor firmly and learn about how your feet work within each pose. Keep socks and a sweatshirt to hand to cover up with before you go into the final Corpse Pose in each session, as this is when your body cools quickly.

when to practice

At first, try to do two or three sessions of at least twenty minutes each week. With time, you'll catch yourself yearning to practice every day or so for up to an hour or two.

First thing in the morning is an excellent time to practice. Your energy is fresh and your yoga will establish good posture and a calm state of mind to help you cope with the day's physical and mental stresses.

After work or before bed, use your yoga as a mental and physical wind-down, allowing you to destress and unknot any tension.

Always wait for a couple of hours after eating before starting your practice.

where to practice

Try to set aside a special yoga space, where you can keep your yoga mat. Having a pleasant place to retreat to without having to shift furniture, ask housemates to move, or turn off the TV, encourages your practice. It might be a corner of the bedroom, part of a home office set-up where you can focus your energies before you start work, or a sheltered spot in the garden.

the equipment you need

It's almost impossible to perform some of the standing poses without a proper sticky yoga mat, available from sports shops, mail order, or gyms. A mat also cushions your knees and sitting bones in sitting and kneeling postures. It's also useful to keep close at hand some firm cushions or bolsters, a foam yoga block (also from sports shops), a towel or wash cloth to wipe away sweat, and a blanket to fold up and cushion knees or support the head.

when not to practice

Don't practice yoga when you have a fever or feel under the weather. And only restart once you feel completely well following a cold or flu. Specific cautions for those with a medical condition, such as high blood pressure or heart disease, are set out in the introduction to each posture, but if you have a medical problem, consult your doctor before starting yoga. Women are advised to avoid strenuous workouts and inverted postures in the heavy days of the menstrual period. If you are pregnant, consult your physician and midwife before starting yoga practice, especially during the first three months. Thereafter, it's best to work with an experienced pregnancy yoga teacher. If you have practiced yoga for some time, it's thought safe to continue poses you are comfortable in, but do not attempt new ones. Avoid backbends, full inversions, and some twists (as indicated in the text).

right > **Yoga practice is easily done at home without any expensive equipment.**

how to use this book

This book presents a series of progressive yoga sessions for the complete beginner, based on the different key movements in yoga: from first work with the spine to standing stretches, bending forward and backward, side stretches and twists, backbends, and inversions. How long you remain at each stage depends on the amount of practice you do, and the dedication with which you approach it. Some people might progress within three weeks; others might prefer to remain on the first session for some months. Take it at a speed at which you feel comfortable; but do keep challenging yourself.

the form of the class

■ **Warm up and breathing:** don't be tempted to skimp on this. Before you start to work on strenuous postures, you need to have warmed up the body's twelve major joints (ankles, knees, hips, wrists, elbows, and shoulders), the large muscles in the arms and legs, and also the body's hardest working muscle, the heart, to enable it to supply working muscles with adequate oxygen. Until you're warm, your tendons and muscles won't be able safely to experience their full range of movement, so injury is more likely. Your co-ordination is also not at its best when you begin: a warm-up starts to link your brain with the activity.

When you start a yoga session, it's important to begin tuning out of your regular life and into where you are and what you want to achieve—this may be toning up, becoming more supple, increasing your sense of well-being, or just having an hour or so to devote to yourself. As you bring your mind to your breathing and begin to co-ordinate your breath with your movements, thoughts concerning your everyday life are forced to take a back seat, and your mind focuses on the room and the present. This in itself is beneficial for relaxation and stress relief.

■ **The poses:** everyone prefers some poses to others. Some are easier physically, some rev

you up mentally; some you look forward to and some you dread. Try to work on each pose in a session equally. Don't shirk the ones you don't like, nor spend extra time in those you find easy. Each of us also favors one side of the body, for right-handed people, usually the right side, which is stronger and often more flexible. The postures in this book always move to the left first, the side of the body that is most often weak. Try to hold each pose for the recommended time on this side before moving on to practice on the other side.

Start each pose slowly, working with attention and goodwill. Hold each pose, even if you hate it, and after a few weeks you will find that you have more strength, greater ability to hold the position, more focused concentration, and a greater lung capacity to accompany your increased flexibility.

■ **Working within a pose:** as you practice, try to fix your mind on the posture. When outside thoughts intrude, as they will, come back to the positioning of your legs and arms, the direction of your gaze, and, above all, to the movement of your breath in and out. Listen to the flow of your breath, and let this fix you in the here and now and erase all other preoccupations. Don't hold your breath in a pose—all too easily done when you are concentrating hard. Breathe into areas of tension, allowing oxygenated blood to help the muscles release, imagining them softening and lengthening, then breathe out the tension with the exhalation. You may find that at the end of the exhalation the muscles give a little, allowing you to inch the pose farther.

■ **Breathing exercises:** at the end of each session before the final relaxation, a breathing exercise or mini-meditation in a sitting or kneeling position starts the full relaxation process before you lie down to relax.

■ **Relaxation:** yoga is especially effective because the body is allowed to rest, adjust, and recuperate after the workout. The poses you have performed will have worked to realign the spine, restore to muscles and joints their full range of movements and, by compressing and releasing, will have acted like acupressure on the internal organs to stimulate and detox. The body needs time to assimilate these changes. Certain poses also work to calm and re-energize the mind, which can cause thoughts and issues to come up. Again, switching the mind off completely in the final relaxation posture allows these thoughts to be assimilated.

left and below > **Always remember to do a warm up before you start your practice to reduce the risk of injuring yourself.**

chapter 2

awakening the spine

- **warming up 20–23**

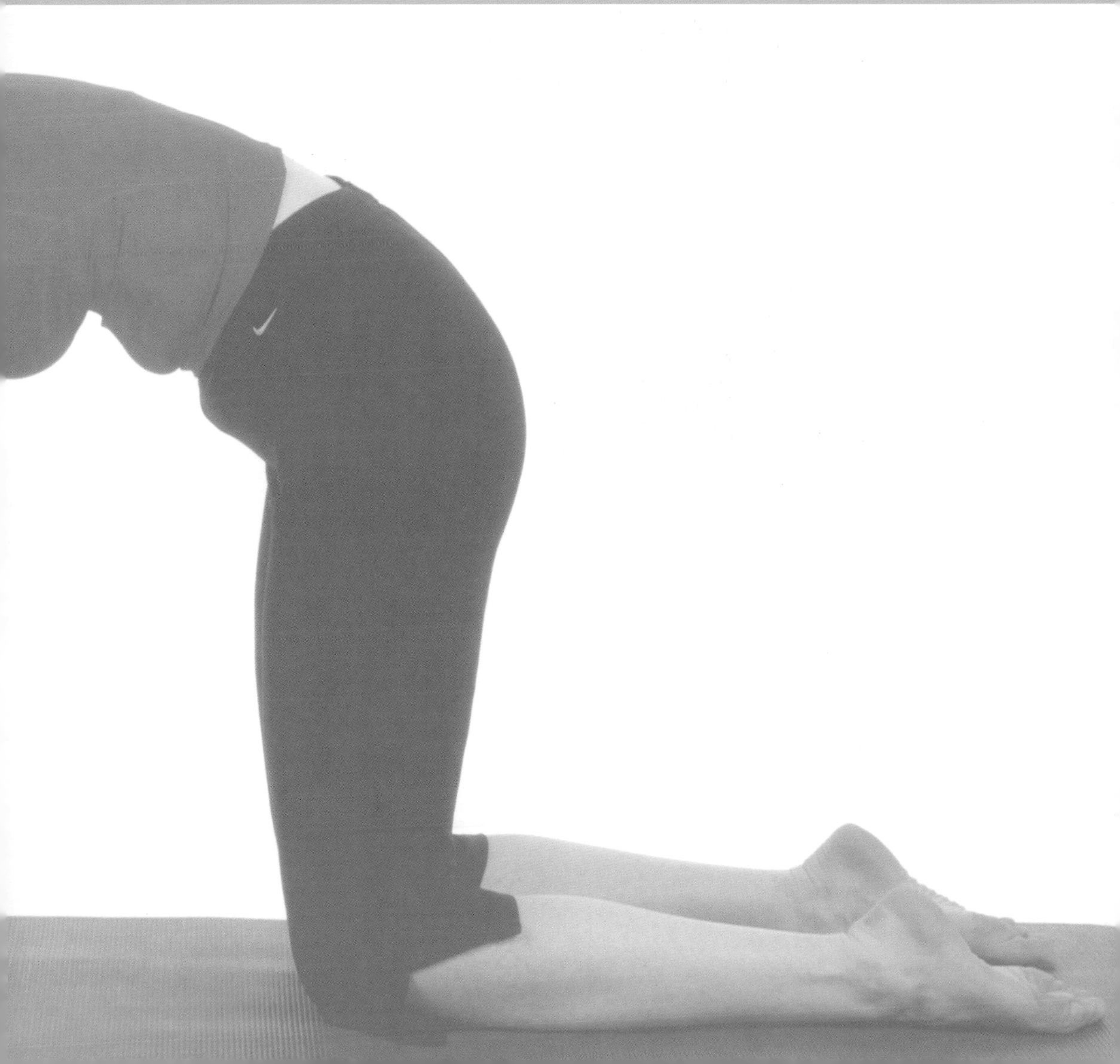

corpse pose with legs bent savasana

Spend 10 to 20 minutes on this warming up, designed to ease out tension, set the foundation for good posture, and counter habitual ways of moving that perpetuate stress patterns. The movements also deepen the breath and bring you into a state of relaxation: once you have let go of your mental preoccupations, you settle into postures more readily.

1 Lie on your back, legs hip-width apart, knees bent, and feet flat on the floor. Rest your arms by your side, slightly away from your body, palms up. Take a few moments to relax.

2 Lift your toes, splay them, hold, then replace on the floor, trying to maintain a gap between each toe. Stretch on to tiptoes, then replace your heels, letting your weight sink down through the base of both big and little toes and the width of both heels.

3 Inhaling, imagine breathing into your pelvis. Feel everything soften and, exhaling, let the bones relax toward the floor. With the out breath, allow the small of your back to drop. Repeat a few times.

4 Breathe in and focus on your shoulderblades, feeling the upper back widen and soften as the air fills your lungs. On the exhalation, let the bones and muscles here melt into the floor, and let go of tension. Repeat a few times.

5 On the next out breath, slide your shoulders toward your hips, backs of your arms on the mat. Repeat two or three times. Tuck your chin in slightly and release any remaining tension here, resting your head against the firm support of the floor.

raising knees to chest

1 Without moving your buttocks and hips, and keeping your chest and
pelvis square, bring your knees toward your chest. Wrap your arms
over your upper shins (palms to elbows if possible), and on each
exhalation, draw your knees toward your chest, without raising your
buttocks or crunching your neck and shoulders.

2 Hold for 30 to 60 seconds, keeping
your shoulders moving along the floor
toward your hips on each out breath.
Enjoy the stretch around the buttocks and
hips. Aim, with practice, to achieve a
good compression as the front thighs pull
in against the abdomen.

3 When ready, take your forehead
toward your knees. Try not to tense
your shoulders nor compress your chest.
Hold for up to 30 seconds, pushing your
hips toward the floor with each exhalation
as you inch your forehead and knees
closer together.

head roll and hip rotation

1 Replace the back of your head on the floor. Keeping your legs
pressed toward your chest, slowly roll your head to the left
with an exhalation. Hold for a moment. Inhaling, take your head
back to center. On the next exhalation, repeat to the right.
Repeat to left and right three times.

2 With your head back in the center, rotate your raised legs to the left.
Use your hands to roll your knees in a circle, starting small and
becoming larger. Let your breathing slow and link it with the movement.
Feel every part of your lower back contact the floor, and when you find
areas of tension, ease them out by moving more slowly. Work for 30
seconds, then repeat to the right.

starting to breathe

1 Replace your feet on the floor, and rest your arms by your
sides, palms down. Take a moment to center your feet
comfortably. On an in breath, raise your arms up to the ceiling.

2 Still breathing in, move your arms back and down
behind your head. Aim for your fingernails to
touch the floor lightly as you complete the inhalation.
Don't arch your lower back.

3 Immediately start to exhale, taking your arms up to the ceiling and back
down to the floor by your sides. Let your fingertips touch the floor lightly
as you complete the exhalation, then start another inhalation, raising your
arms up and back as before.

4 Repeat the arm raising with each inhalation and exhalation
for 2 to 3 minutes, creating one continuous flow as the
movement of your arms reflects your breathing pattern. Take
your focus to your abdomen, watching it expand as you breathe
in and contract toward your lower back as you breathe out.

forward bend to a wall ardha uttanasana

beginner

When you bend forward from a standing position, you work first to establish a straight spine, and from this foundation, move on to fold the body in half. In this session, you focus on the first part of the movement only to increase flexibility not just in the spine, but in the hip joints and hamstring muscles, where the forward-bending action begins. You will need a wall: stand facing it so that when you bend forward, your hands reach flat to the wall and your hips remain over your ankles.

1 Place your feet hip-width apart, with the outer edges parallel. Look at how your bodyweight bears down through your feet. Distribute your weight evenly between your right and left feet, and between your big and little toes and both sides of the heels.

2 Check your stability by swaying forward and back and from side to side until you find a point just forward from your heels at which you gain an effortless lift. Inhaling, extend up from this point, pulling up from your inner ankles, lifting your kneecaps, and tucking your tailbone in and up slightly to extend your lower back. Check that your shoulders, hips, knees, and ankles are aligned. Lift out of your pelvis, broadening your chest.

3 Inhaling, take your arms overhead, shoulders relaxing away from your ears, fingertips inching toward the ceiling, palms facing forward. Hold for a couple of breaths.

4 Exhaling, pivot from the hips to stretch forward, taking your fingertips, then palms flat to the wall. Aim to make an inverted L-shape with your legs and back: shuffle your feet in or out until your hips align with your ankles and your back is perfectly straight. Check that your hips align and your hands and shoulders are level. Hold for 30 to 60 seconds, enjoying a stretch from palms to hips and feeling the back of the thighs lengthen. If the hamstrings are tight, work for a few sessions with knees slightly bent. Pivot from the hips to come up.

precautions

■ Don't progress to the full Standing Forward Bend (see pages 106–107) until you feel comfortable in this pose.

benefits boosts flexibility in the hips, legs, and spine ● strengthens the knees ● rests the heart and lungs ● tones up the abdomen ● calms the mind ● relieves fatigue ● rejuvenates the brain

standing wheel pose utthita chakrasana

Yoga complements one movement with its opposite to maintain equilibrium. So this posture counterposes the standing forward bend with a standing backward bend. This stretch again helps you focus on elongating the length of the spine before you start to bend. It then stretches as a long fluid unit rather than only in the areas that naturally bend backward and damage easiest—the back of the waist and neck. If you feel pinching in the lower back, come up, re-establish the standing extension in steps 1 and 2, then start again.

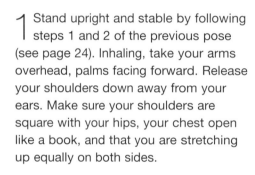

1 Stand upright and stable by following steps 1 and 2 of the previous pose (see page 24). Inhaling, take your arms overhead, palms facing forward. Release your shoulders down away from your ears. Make sure your shoulders are square with your hips, your chest open like a book, and that you are stretching up equally on both sides.

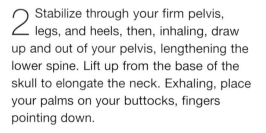

2 Stabilize through your firm pelvis, legs, and heels, then, inhaling, draw up and out of your pelvis, lengthening the lower spine. Lift up from the base of the skull to elongate the neck. Exhaling, place your palms on your buttocks, fingers pointing down.

3 Start lifting your upper back as if bringing it forward into your chest. At the same time roll your shoulders back and open the chest, lengthening from pubic bone to chin. Lift your chin to take your head gently back without crunching the back of the neck. Pull your elbows in and inch your palms toward the back of your knees. Hold for 20 to 30 seconds, arching further with each exhalation, and opening the chest with each inhalation. Come back to vertical on an inhalation.

4 When you feel confident, extend back with arms overhead, ears in line with your arms, without losing length in the lower back and neck. Focus on extending up and out rather than dropping back.

precautions

■ Be careful not to take any strain in the lower back or back of the neck; avoid during pregnancy.

benefits strengthens and increases flexibility in the spine ● works the lower back ● opens the chest ● enhances kidney function ● releases energy ● lifts the spirits

standing twist

beginner

A simple twist from standing, this stretch rotates the spine from its base to bring fresh blood to the spinal cord, and leads to a sense of recharging and rejuvenation. The mobility needed to rotate declines with age, so to slow the ageing process, make twists a daily habit. Don't push this movement though—doing so can lead to injury. Go only as far as your body will allow, then focus on breathing and stretching upward in the pose rather than turning further.

1 Stand with toes and heels together, hips and shoulders level and facing forward, shoulderblades coming together, and shoulders releasing away from the ears. Look forward.

2 Step your right foot over your left so the outer edges of both feet touch, toes and heels level. Pull up, compressing the inner thighs together. Work to keep the pelvis facing forward and hips level.

3 Raise your arms to shoulder level, palms down, stretching out as if reaching out to both sides of the room. Keep your shoulders relaxed, and extend up the back of the neck to raise the crown of your head toward the ceiling.

4 Maintaining your arm position, turn your entire trunk to face left. Anchor in the inner edge of your left foot, and pull your buttocks together to keep your pelvis facing forward and maintain stability. Don't let your right arm veer too far forward; broaden your chest instead. Turn your head to look along your left middle finger.

5 Hold for 30 to 60 seconds. With each inhalation extend your spine. With each exhalation, focus on the twist, seeing if you can turn a little further with your hips facing forward. Come back to center on an inhalation, countertwist to the right for a few seconds, unfold your legs, and repeat on the other side.

benefits boosts flexibility in the hips and upper back • frees up the pelvis • relieves lower back pain • boosts the digestive system • eases constipation • energizes

cat pose bilikasana

beginner

In Cat Pose, the spine undulates in a lovely stretch that reaches every vertebra. This version includes a variation that elongates the spine by compressing and extending from side to side, too. Co-ordinate your breath with the movements, inhaling as you raise the chest, and exhaling as you arch the upper spine in one fluid cycle.

1 Start on hands and knees, legs hip-width apart, shoulders over wrists, and knees under hips. Look down so the spine is aligned from its base to the crown of the head like a table top.

2 Exhaling, tuck your pelvis under. Draw your abdominal muscles toward your lower back as you curve your middle spine upward. Press through your wrists to take the upper back toward the ceiling without crunching your shoulders. Finally, and on the same exhalation, relax your forehead toward your chest to feel the entire spine form an upward arc.

3 On the next inhalation, reverse the stretch. Uncurl your pelvis, letting your abdomen and lower back drop (without compressing the lower back), lengthen your middle back forward, and, pressing through your wrists, broaden your chest forward and up. Finally, and on the same inhalation, lift your chin toward the ceiling.

4 Repeat the upward curve on the next exhalation, working for 1 to 2 minutes and linking the movements with your breath. Come back to the table-top starting position, balancing your bodyweight equally through your hands, knees, and feet.

5 On the next exhalation, take your left ear toward your left hip, feeling a stretch along your right side. Do not twist; keep the stretch on one plane.

6 Inhale back to center, then repeat on the next exhalation to the other side, taking your right ear to your right hip. Keep looking down throughout. Repeat for 1 to 2 minutes. Relax back on your heels.

precautions

■ If you have back problems, do not look up in step 3; instead, keep the top of the head stretching away from the base of the spine, forming a table-top shape.

benefits increases flexibility in every part of the spine • strengthens the pelvis • works the wrists and arms

cobbler pose baddha konasana

beginner

Don't neglect the abdominals when working on the spine. Various sets of abdominal muscles keep the pelvis in its correct position, stabilizing movements such as twisting, bending, and lifting, and minimizing the possibility of injury. Working the spine without strengthening these muscles can put strain on the lower back. Cobbler Pose engages the abdominals to support the lower back and because you work from a stable seated position, you don't have to worry about tired leg muscles. This posture also strengthens your arms: the support of the arms gives you the power to open the chest and stretch upward.

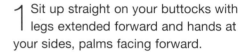

1 Sit up straight on your buttocks with legs extended forward and hands at your sides, palms facing forward.

2 Spread your legs wide. Pull out any excess flesh from beneath your sitting bones. Replace your hands, and extend your spine up out of the pelvis.

3 Bend at the knees to bring your feet together near your groin. Interlock your fingers and firmly grasp your toes. Exhaling, stretch your spine, drawing your abdominal muscles back, stretching through both sides of the body equally, and lifting through the back of the neck. Keeping this feeling of lift, press your feet together to work your knees toward the floor, broadening your chest, rolling your shoulders back and away from your ears, and using the firmness of your arms to support the extension.

benefits improves posture
● promotes all-round flexibility
● tones the abdominal and arm muscles ● helps guard against arthritis of the knees, hips, and pelvis
● regulates the menstrual cycle

4 Hold for 30 to 60 seconds. With each in breath extend upward, lengthening the whole waist. With each inhalation work your knees down toward the floor. Feel a three-way movement up through the spine, down through the knees, and opening in the chest.

inverted lake pose viparita karani

beginner

Many schools of yoga end work on poses with an inverted posture. In this easy version of an inversion, you relax with your legs resting against a wall, spine supported by the floor as you benefit from the restorative effects of boosted circulation to the upper body. Most inversions are not recommended for women during menstruation, but this pose is safe at any time of the month.

1 Sit with your buttocks and back pressing against a wall, legs outstretched. Swivel to one side, one buttock still in contact with the wall, and bend your knees, feet flat to the floor.

2 Turn on to your back with both buttocks touching the wall. Take your legs one by one up the wall, knees slightly bent. Relax your arms to the side, palms open and facing upward, and let your chest widen downward. Feel your shoulders giving their weight to the floor. Work to straighten the legs with each out breath, pressing through the heels and both edges of the feet, as if supporting a weight on the soles.

3 If desired, inhale and stretch your arms above your chest. Hold, relaxing the shoulders and small of the back into the mat, then lower your arms to rest behind your head. With each out breath work to release the back of your neck and lower back downward. With each in breath feel your shoulderblades spreading outward and shoulders moving toward your hips. Hold for 2 to 3 minutes. Reverse the movements you used to get into the pose to exit it.

benefits relieves exhaustion ● eases migraine and stress-related headaches ● soothes indigestion ● prevents varicose veins ● calms and rejuvenates

progressive muscle relaxation in corpse pose savasana

All yoga sessions end with relaxation in the Corpse Pose, which allows the benefits of the stretches to be assimilated and relaxes you completely. Although it might seem physically easy, this posture is famed as the most difficult yoga pose to accomplish, since it involves freeing the mind from thoughts. One way toward such total relaxation is this physical letting-go exercise, which allows you to appreciate the sensation of relaxation by contrasting it with the experience of tension. You might like to cushion your head or the backs of your knees with a folded towel or pillow.

1 Lie on your back, legs hip-width apart extending away from you, feet and knees dropping outward. Relax your arms away from your sides so that both shoulderblades are flat to the floor. Place your palms up and loosely open. Lift your head, look toward your toes to align it with your body, then replace it on the mat, chin tucked in slightly to stretch the back of the neck. Close your eyes.

2 Tense and relax every part of the body in turn. Start at the toes and feet: clench the muscles in every part of the left foot tightly, lifting it a few inches, then releasing to the floor. Feel the solid weight of your relaxed foot on the floor. Work upward, tightening and releasing your left calf and thigh, then repeat on the right leg. Feel the heaviness of your completely relaxed legs.

3 Tense your buttocks, gripping them and lifting slightly. Hold, then release to the floor. Next, compress and hold in your abdomen and chest. Let them relax, soften, and spread.

4 Tense your whole left arm; clench the hand into a fist, then extend the fingers. Feel the arm shake with tension. Let the arm drop heavily to the ground, totally relaxed. Repeat on the right arm. Now tense your shoulders, pulling them tightly up and into the neck. Hold, retaining your breath for as long as possible, then let everything go as you exhale. Release into the mat.

5 Screw up your face, pursing your mouth, furrowing your forehead, screwing up your eyes, and contracting your ears. Then yawn widely, opening your eyes and ears. Release, letting go of any gripping in the jaw, forehead, and mouth. Relax your tongue, ears, nostrils, and the back of your scalp. Close your eyes again.

6 Scan your body from the toes up. Where you find areas of residual tension, ask the tension to dissolve and let that part of the body melt into the floor. Picture every part of your body softening and spreading outward and down, giving itself further to the firm support of the floor with each exhalation.

7 Focus on deepening your breath, watching it move in and out. As thoughts intrude, acknowledge them, then return to watching your breath. Remain in the pose for 5 to 10 minutes.

8 Stretch before bending your knees, turning to the right, and resting for a few moments. Sit up slowly, head last.

benefits relaxes the body ● regulates blood pressure ● develops powers of concentration ● promotes feelings of inner peace ● relieves stress

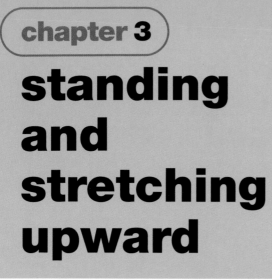

neck roll and shoulder shrug

This standing warm-up releases accumulated tension and constriction, lubricates the major joints, and brings warmth and energy to the large muscles.

1 Stand comfortably, hips aligned over knees and ankles, shoulders over hips, arms and hands relaxed by your side. Exhaling, take your chin down and into your throat, compressing the thyroid.

2 Inhaling, pivot your head to point your chin at the ceiling, feeling the stretch in your throat. Exhale back to center.

3 On an exhalation, drop your left ear to your left shoulder. Start the stretch in the base of your spine and extend it up and over. Inhale to center; repeat to the right.

4 Exhaling, tuck your chin in, parallel to the floor, feeling a lift up the back of the skull. Inhale and take your chin forward, like a tortoise. Exhale to center.

5 Inhaling, pivot your head to look left. Exhale and look behind your shoulder. Inhale back to center, and exhale. Repeat to the right.

6 Make a couple of large, slow circles with your head clockwise, then anticlockwise. Work extra slowly where you still find areas of tension.

7 Bring your shoulders up to your ears on an inhalation. Hold the breath, squeezing the muscles tightly, then release on the exhalation. Repeat.

hip, knee, and ankle circle

1 Place your hands on your hips and make large clockwise circles with your hips. Exaggerate the movement, taking your hips out far to the front, right to the back, and out to each side. Make two or three circles, then repeat in the other direction. Complete with some figure-of-eight movements.

2 Bend your knees and place your palms over your kneecaps. Pressing firmly, rotate the kneecaps away from each other and around to make an outward circle two or three times. Don't worry if the knees click. Repeat, circling inward.

3 Stand upright and lift your left knee. Keeping the lower and upper leg immobile, point your toes and, imagining your big toe is a pencil, rotate at the ankle joint to draw a circle the size of a plate on the floor. Isolate the movement in the ankle. Make two or three circles clockwise, then change direction. Repeat with the right leg.

mountain pose tadasana

beginner

When the body's major joints are aligned in the key standing posture of hatha yoga, Mountain Pose, the skeletal system exists in a state of ease, reducing stress, empowering you with strength, and allowing a fresh sense of freedom to invigorate your posture. Make this pose your foundation in every standing pose

1 Stand with big toes and heels touching. Establish a base: lift your toes, splay them, then replace on the floor, trying to maintain a gap between each toe. Shift your bodyweight so it is equal between both feet, and on each foot equal between the base of the big and little toes and the full width of both heels. Lift through your ankles, pulling up through the inner legs, and draw your kneecaps and thigh muscles up and in.

2 Pull up through both hips, making sure they are centered over your knees. Bring your buttocks together without gripping, and tuck your pelvis slightly up and under to lengthen your lower back. Draw your abdomen back and up as you extend up to your armpits.

3 Broaden your chest and relax your shoulders away from your ears, rolling your shoulderblades toward each other. Keep your shoulders centered over your hips. Stretch your arms down by your sides, palms facing inward.

benefits establishes good posture • lengthens out the spine • focuses the concentration • tones the buttocks and the thighs

4 Tuck your chin toward your throat, parallel to the floor. Imagine a string at the crown of your head pulling you toward the ceiling. Hold for 30 to 60 seconds, breathing extension into the upper body as you inhale, and letting each exhalation ground your lower body through your heels.

tree pose vrkasana

beginner

In Tree Pose, you retain the stability of Mountain Pose while lengthening the spine and reaching for the sky. This posture is one of the balances—vital postures that train your focus and bring you into the present for increased mental clarity. Take your attention to one point at eye-level as you work; remember that if your mind wavers, your body will follow.

1 Stand in Mountain Pose (see pages 44–45) with feet hip-width apart. Shift your weight on to your left foot, and pause to regain your stability. Lift your right foot and press the sole into the inner ankle, calf, or thigh of the standing leg, knee outward and hips level and open.

2 Take a little time to re-establish your stability. Then pull up through the standing leg and, tucking your abdomen in and up, lengthen your torso. Broaden your chest as if opening a book. Lengthen your spine out of the pelvis and tuck your chin in slightly as you lift out of the back of the skull: imagine a string at the crown of the head. Look forward, fixing your gaze on one point.

3 When you feel strong and aligned in the standing leg, bring your fingers and palms together in prayer position in front of your chest. Focus your breathing here for a while.

4 Inhaling, extend your arms overhead, forearms and palms coming toward each other, shoulders releasing down, away from your ears. Lift out of the hip of the standing leg.

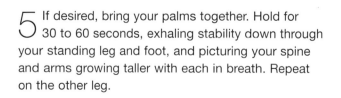

5 If desired, bring your palms together. Hold for 30 to 60 seconds, exhaling stability down through your standing leg and foot, and picturing your spine and arms growing taller with each in breath. Repeat on the other leg.

benefits tones the leg muscles
● strengthens the ankles
● establishes balance ● helps to focus the concentration

extended triangle pose

utthita trikonasana

beginner

This dynamic standing stretch increases flexibility in the trunk, legs, and spine. In Extended Triangle Pose, you start working with legs separated. This foundation broadens your pelvis, allowing you to stretch upright effectively, while toning the muscles of the legs, and activating the stabilizing power of the feet.

1 Stand in Mountain Pose (see pages 44–45). Inhaling, jump or step your feet 3 to 4ft apart, with the outer edges of your feet parallel. Adjust your bodyweight so it is balanced on both feet. Extend up through the inner legs. Center your pelvis, tuck your abdomen up and back, broaden your chest, and lengthen the spine out of the back of your skull. Extend your arms parallel to the floor, palms down.

2 Turn your left foot and thigh out 90°, your right foot in slightly. Pull your buttocks toward each other and rotate the thighs toward their buttocks to provide support. Anchor in the outer edge of the back foot.

3 Inhaling, raise your right arm and extend your torso left, keeping the extension on one plane. Bring your left hand to your calf, ankle, or, as you progress, the floor without collapsing the left side of your torso. Reach to the ceiling, rolling your top ribs out and drawing your fingertips up. Look at your top thumb. If you wish, support your lower hand on a block or thick book.

4 Hold for 30 to 60 seconds, grasping your big toe, if desired. With each inhalation, stretch from fingertips to fingertips, and lengthen from the base of the spine to the crown. Keep your bodyweight bearing down through your front heel. Inhale to come up. Repeat to the other side.

precautions

■ If you feel dizzy turning the head up, keep looking down in step 3.

benefits strengthens the legs and ankles ● tones the pelvis ● prevents stooping shoulders ● soothes backache ● eases menstrual pain

warrior pose II virabhadrasana II

Test your new-found stability, spinal strength, and confidence of posture with this powerful standing pose. In Warrior II, you embody the qualities of a fighter—strength, confidence, poise, and purposeful power. This pose can be quite challenging at first; aim to hold it as long as you can with control and calmness. When it all gets too much, stop, take a rest, then try once more. After a few weeks' practice, the movements will become effortless.

1 Stand in Mountain Pose (see pages 44–45). Inhaling, jump or step your feet a good 3 to 4ft (90 to 120cm) apart. Make sure the outer edges of your feet are parallel. Adjust your bodyweight so it is balanced between both feet. Extend up through the inner legs. Center your pelvis, tuck your abdomen up and back, broaden your chest, and lengthen the spine out of the back of your skull. Extend your arms parallel to the floor, palms down.

2 Turn your left foot and thigh out 90°, your right foot in slightly. Pull your buttocks toward each other, and subtly rotate your weight outward on both feet to anchor your legs.

3 Exhale and bend your left knee to make a right angle. Sink your pelvis, aiming to have your thigh parallel to the floor. Keep your weight evenly balanced between both legs and your hips opening. Lengthen up from this stable base.

4 Turn your head to look along your left arm at your middle finger. Hold for 30 to 60 seconds. With each inhalation, lengthen the spine and extend the arms, chest and shoulderblades broadening. With each exhalation, anchor through the outer edge of the back foot. Inhale as you straighten the bent leg, then repeat to the other side.

benefits builds strength in the upper and lower body • increases stamina • tones the hips • keeps the knees and hips flexible • eases lower backache • soothes stiff shoulders

precautions

■ Avoid if you are suffering from any heart condition.

warrior pose I virabhadrasana I

advancing beginner

Continue the vigorous standing poses with the upward lift of this more challenging Warrior Pose, which boosts your sense of achievement while building strength in the spine and shoulders. Complete beginners might like to work on the previous Warrior Pose (see page 50) for a few weeks before moving on to this more intense posture.

1 Stand in Mountain Pose (see pages 44–45). Inhaling, jump or step your feet a good 3 to 4ft (90 to 120cm) apart. Make sure the outer edges of your feet are parallel. Adjust your bodyweight so it is balanced between both feet. Extend up through the inner legs from ankles to thighs. Center your pelvis, tuck your abdomen up and back, broaden your chest, and lengthen the spine out of the back of your skull. Extend your arms parallel to the floor, palms down.

2 Turn your left foot and thigh out 90°, then pivot your right foot so your right hip faces forward, torso square to the wall in front of you.

3 Bend your front knee over the ankle, taking the thigh parallel to the floor. Extend the spine. Inhaling, take your arms overhead, palms facing each other, fingertips reaching up. Lengthen through your back ribs, keeping your torso square.

4 If you are flexible in the upper back, bring your palms together in prayer position, without raising the shoulders. Look at your palms.

5 If desired, gently drop your head back by pointing your chin at the ceiling. Hold for 30 to 60 seconds, stretching both sides of the body up from the firm anchor of your pelvis, and feeling your back leg anchored from heel to thigh. Inhale to come up, and repeat to the other side.

precautions

■ Avoid if you have high blood pressure or a heart condition.

benefits expands the chest, increasing lung capacity • tones the abdominals • keeps the knees and thighs flexible • strengthens the spine • works the arms • boosts the digestive system

intense leg stretch
prasarita padottanasana

`beginner`

This standing forward bend with wide legs completes the work on dynamic standing postures by offering all the benefits of an inversion while continuing to work the thighs and hips. The spine is completely relaxed as a brisk flow of blood to the head invigorates the brain and the heart, and the lungs are exercised. Simultaneously, you start to relax and experience a sense of tranquillity.

1 Stand in Mountain Pose (see pages 44–45). Inhaling, jump or step your feet a good 3 to 4ft (90 to 120cm) apart. Make sure the outer edges of your feet are parallel. Adjust your bodyweight so it is balanced between both feet. Extend up through the inner legs. Center your pelvis, tuck your abdomen up and back, broaden your chest, and lengthen the spine out of the back of your skull. Inhaling, raise your arms overhead, dropping your shoulders away from your ears. Hold the lovely stretch from ankles to fingertips. Look up if desired.

benefits works the heart and lungs
● tones the abdominal muscles
● strengthens the ankles ● lengthens
the hamstrings ● reduces blood
pressure ● restorative for the brain

precautions

■ Do not compress your neck at any stage of the posture.

2 Exhaling, extend forward, pivoting from the hips and maintaining the stretch along the entire length of the spine. Place your fingertips or palms flat on the floor in line with your toes. Check that your weight is bearing down through your heels and your buttocks are extending up to the ceiling. Relax your spine, bend your elbows, and relax your neck and shoulders. Do not bounce. If you wish, support your head on a bolster placed between your feet.

3 Hold for 30 to 60 seconds, releasing the spine, calves, and backs of the thighs with each exhalation. If you have enough flexibility, take the crown of your head to rest between your palms. Do not compress the back of your neck. Let each exhalation pull the abdomen in and up to increase the extension in the back and legs. Inhale to come up gradually, bringing your head up last.

deep breathing sitting
cross-legged pranayama in sukhasana

beginner

Breathing is the essence of yoga. As you work with the postures, you learn to focus on deepening and slowing the flow of oxygen in and out of the body. This helps you let go of muscular tension and release into the movement. At the same time, it blocks out all other thoughts, increasing your concentration and dissolving mental tension. In this pose, you start to think about how you breathe habitually, which will help you to achieve a more effective breathing pattern. Each time you practice, change the cross of your legs.

precautions

■ If you have high blood pressure or heart problems, work with an experienced yoga teacher.

1 Sit with legs outstretched, then open them wide. Bend your knees, crossing your right shin over your left. Sit up straight, extending out of your pelvis and feeling your sitting bones firmly rooted. If you find it impossible to sit cross-legged with a straight spine, sit with your lower back supported by a wall. If this, too, is unbearable, sit on a firm chair with your feet flat on the floor. As you practice over the weeks, work toward sitting unsupported on the floor.

benefits sitting cross-legged is restful, increases flexibility in the hips, strengthens the knees, and improves circulation in the legs and feet ● deep breathing regulates blood pressure, boosts oxygen intake, detoxifies the blood, calms and focuses, and is regenerative for body and mind

2 Place one palm on your chest, the other flat on your abdomen. Close your eyes and start to watch your breathing. Notice which hand moves. If it's the upper hand, you're shallow-breathing and not benefiting from a full in breath.

3 Place both hands low on your abdomen, one on each side. As you breathe in, imagine the breath dropping toward the abdomen, causing your fingertips to draw away from each other and the back of your waist and rib cage to expand. Imagine this as a balloon inflating from the bottom up.

4 As you exhale, picture the breath leaving the balloon in your abdomen little by little from the top down and notice how your fingertips touch again. This is one breath cycle. Take a regular breath, if necessary, then repeat the cycle for up to 3 minutes, picturing the imaginary balloon inflating and deflating.

tension-release in corpse pose

savasana

beginner

As you sink into Corpse Pose at the end of this session, use the time to sense how different your body feels. You might experience an energized tingling in your palms or fingers, a freedom of the neck and shoulders, or a sense of invigoration in the large muscles of the legs. Relish these changes: proof that your body is toning up and your mind is becoming able to relax at will. In this session, you work in Corpse Pose to let go of physical tension.

1 Lie on your back, legs hip-width apart and extending away from you, feet and knees dropping outward. Relax your arms away from your sides so that both shoulderblades are flat to the floor. Place your palms up and loosely open. Lift your head only, look toward your toes to align it with your body, then replace on the mat, chin tucked in slightly to extend the back of the neck. Close your eyes.

2 Use the muscle-relaxation technique on pages 36–37 to tense and relax every part of the body. Start at the toes and work up to the skull, each time allowing the body part to sink into the floor, and letting go of any ingrained patterns of tension that have built up over the years.

3 When you have relaxed every part of the body in turn, scan your body from the toes up. You might find residual tension around your lower back, your shoulders, or solar plexus area.

4 Visualize a tiny hole centered at the base of your spine. Picture the tension you have found turning into liquid and making its way slowly to this tiny hole at the base of your spine. As you exhale, let the stream of tension drip away. Work on this technique for a while, allowing it to erase all other thoughts.

precautions

■ If you are pregnant or have a respiratory disorder, raise your chest by placing a cushion beneath it; if you have lower back problems, keep your knees bent, feet flat on the floor.

5 When you feel totally relaxed physically, take your focus to your breath. Watch it move in and out, and see how the out breath naturally lengthens and the in breath is completely involuntary. Give in to this process as you rest in the pose for 5 to 10 minutes.

6 Wiggle your fingers and toes, stroking your fingertips against your palms a few times. Stretch your arms and legs, bend your knees, then roll onto your right side to rest for a few moments before sitting up.

benefits relaxes the body
● regulates blood pressure ● relieves stress ● develops concentration
● promotes feelings of inner peace

bending forward and back

chest expander

Begin by mobilizing the major joints, following the routine set out on pages 40–43. Then let this chest- and lung-opening exercise warm up the large muscles in the arms and legs, and stretch the entire spine as you start consciously to synchronize your breathing pattern with your movements.

1 Standing tall with feet hip-width apart, bring your hands to your chest, fingertips touching, palms facing forward, elbows out.

2 As you start to inhale, push your palms forward, extending the arms and holding the stretch briefly through the wrists.

3 Still inhaling, sweep your outstretched arms to the sides and behind you. Interlock your fingers by your buttocks and pull downward and back slightly to stretch your arms and shoulders. Feel your chest opening and, at the end of the inhalation, tip your head back, chin pointing up. Don't collapse in the small of the back.

4 As you start to exhale, pivot forward from the hips, relaxing your head and shoulders as they drop toward the ground. Feel your buttocks lengthening toward the ceiling as your weight travels down through your heels. Extend your still-interlocked hands upward, backs of the hands to the ceiling. Hold, relaxing the backs of the legs, neck, and shoulders as you exhale completely.

5 Inhale as you pivot back to standing. Unclasp your hands as you exhale, bringing them back in front of your chest ready to begin the movement again with the next inhalation. Repeat 5 to 7 times, building up a flowing movement that co-ordinates naturally with your breathing. Each time, interlock your fingers with the opposite thumb on top.

downward facing dog pose
adho mukha svanasana

beginner

One of many people's favorite yoga stretches, the dynamic Downward Facing Dog Pose is a good way to boost your agility and energy at the start of a session. It warms up the back of the body by providing every part with a good stretch—heels, hamstrings, the length of the spine, shoulders, arms, and wrists. It also strengthens the ankles and legs to prepare for standing postures, and offers the calming benefits of an inversion, helping the brain relax in preparation for the yoga class.

1 Start on hands and knees, legs hip-width apart and creating right angles with your hips and legs, and shoulders and arms. Draw in your abdominal muscles and look down so the spine resembles a flat table top. Turn your toes under.

2 Exhaling and keeping your knees slightly bent, press on your palms to lift your hips high. Rise up on tip toes, stretching through the arches of your feet, and press your sitting bones to the ceiling. Lengthen out of your shoulders.

3 Straighten your legs as much as possible, pressing your heels toward the ground. If your hamstrings are tight, roll up a towel or place a block beneath your heels. Relax your neck and head, draw out of the shoulders, and widen your shoulderblades. Hold for 30 to 60 seconds, simultaneously extending into the heels, out of the shoulders, and toward the ceiling. Come back to hands and knees on an exhalation, then sink your buttocks back on your heels and rest.

benefits tones the legs • strengthens the ankles
• lengthens the hamstrings • releases crunched shoulders
• energizes • restorative for the brain and nervous system

upward facing dog pose
urdhva mukha svanasana

advancing beginner

This pose complements the last: where Downward Dog stretches the back side of the body from heels to wrists, this posture extends your front. In doing so, it energizes the toes, front of thighs, abdomen, chest, and throat, and boosts circulation. You may find the strain on your arms and wrists hard at first if your upper body is not used to exercise. Persevere—if you practice this pose every other day for two weeks, it magically becomes achievable.

1 Lie prone with legs outstretched and hip-width apart, forehead on the floor and arms by your sides. Bend your elbows and take your palms beneath your shoulders, fingers facing forward, elbows pressing toward your waist.

2 Exhaling, turn your toes under and try to lift your body about an inch off the floor, keeping it completely straight, balanced between your toes and palms. Hold briefly. If impossible, keep your knees on the floor.

precautions

■ If you have tight ankles or feet, or feel any pinching in your lower back, work with your knees on the floor.

benefits develops the arms and shoulders • opens the chest • strengthens weak knees • aligns the legs and knees • boosts circulation

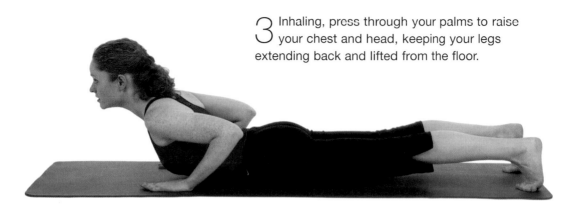

3 Inhaling, press through your palms to raise your chest and head, keeping your legs extending back and lifted from the floor.

4 Straighten your arms to lift your trunk. Bring your pelvis forward and stretch up through your torso, lifting and broadening your chest, and taking your shoulders toward your lower back without compressing it. Finally, point your chin to the ceiling to take your head gently back. Try to hold for 30 seconds, bending your arms on an exhalation to come down with control. Relax on your front for a few minutes.

staff pose dandasana

beginner

The foundation position for good forward bending, Staff Pose is especially useful for those who sit for long periods at a desk, since it brings dynamism to the length of the spine and tones the legs while improving your sitting posture.

1 Sit with legs outstretched, arms by your sides, palms pressing down by your hips, fingers pointing forward. Pivot forward and pull out excess flesh from beneath your sitting bones. Replace the palms of your hands.

2 Exhaling, lengthen your legs along the floor by pressing through the back of your thighs, calves, and heels, pushing out equally through the inside and outside edges of your feet.

3 Inhaling, lift your spine out of your pelvis, stretching each side equally. Open your chest, bring your shoulderblades together, pull your chin toward your throat, and stretch up through the back of your skull to the ceiling. Hold for 30 seconds or longer.

head to knee pose janu sirsasana

beginner

The first forward bend you encounter, Head to Knee Pose stretches the back of the legs, arms, shoulders, and hips while extending and rotating the spine. As you work, aim to pivot forward over the hips and lengthen the spine rather than rounding the back to get the head down. This will give you the suppleness you need in the hamstrings for successful forward bending. Being realistic may take the pressure off: it could take many months' practice before your head finally reaches your calves.

1 Sit in Staff Pose (see opposite), then open your legs wide.

2 Bend your right knee and bring the heel to rest in front of your pubic bone, your right big toe touching your left inner thigh. Let the bent knee relax toward the floor, and keep the extended leg straight, knee facing the ceiling, toes pointing upward.

precautions

■ If you find it difficult at first to keep the spine straight, practice against a wall to give you support.

3 Sit upright, lifting out of the pelvis and squaring your shoulders over your hips. Feel the crown of your head moving toward the ceiling. Inhaling, extend your arms overhead, growing taller without tensing your shoulders. Press the bent knee down. Rotate so your torso is square over your left thigh. Take a few breaths.

4 Exhaling, pivot forward from your hips, arms still extending as if reaching out to the opposite corner of the room, neck and shoulders relaxed.

5 Keeping the extension in your lower back, drop your hands to the floor on either side of your extended leg, and with each out breath push from the lower back to take your torso forward, then down. As you exhale, drop both thighs to the floor and push out through both edges of the outstretched foot.

6 If you have the flexibility, grab your left foot with your hands (eventually aim to grasp your right wrist with your left fingers beyond the sole of the foot). If not, keep stretching forward from your navel with each inhalation and relaxing downward with every exhalation. Work for 30 to 60 seconds, aiming to rest your abdomen, chest, and forehead in that order onto your outstretched leg. Come up on an inhalation, turn back to center, and repeat to the other side.

benefits strengthens the chest muscles ● tones the abdominals ● works the leg muscles ● boosts stability

variation
■ If you wish, at Step 6, place a bolster on your outstretched leg and recline forward onto it.

camel pose ushtrasana

advancing beginner

This is the first backbend in the program. The opening it gives the chest, shoulders, throat, and abdomen can bring a sense of freedom and awakening to an area that is commonly constricted by slouching forward for long periods. For effective backbending you need to stretch the front of the thighs to prevent compression in the lower back. This pose does the work admirably, making it a good preparation for the more intense backbends later in the book. If you find the final pose too challenging, remain at step 2 until you gain the flexibility to ease backward without strain.

precautions

■ Avoid if you have high blood pressure and during pregnancy.

1 Kneel up with legs hip-width apart and perpendicular to the floor, feet parallel with each other. Lift through the thighs and pelvis, making a straight line from knees to ears. Look forward and raise your arms overhead.

2 Drop your hands to your buttocks, fingers downward. Exhaling, keep the upward extension from knees to crown, then start to lengthen back, as if dropping over the top of the spine. Extend the stretch into the back of the neck. Inhaling, open the chest further. If the lower back feels compressed, straighten up and begin again. Push your buttocks and thighs forward slightly. Press down through the palms, opening and releasing the chest.

3 When ready, take back one, then the other hand to cup each heel. Keep your hips moving forward to retain the right angle with the floor. Carefully drop your head to look behind.

4 If you are flexible enough, press your palms firmly into your soles. Hold for 30 seconds or more; inhale back to upright, then immediately sink your buttocks to your heels as in Child Pose (see pages 74–75).

benefits lengthens the front thighs ● stretches the pelvis and lower back ● eases stiff shoulders ● expands the chest and ribs for easier deep breathing ● boosts blood flow around the spine ● improves posture

child pose balasana

beginner

Adopt this relaxed pose for rest and recuperation after backbends, since it arches the spine in the opposite direction. Use it as an antidote whenever your yoga practice becomes too strenuous, or you just want a little time-out.

1 Kneel with your buttocks on your heels, palms on your thighs. Inhaling, straighten your spine, pulling your abdominal muscles in to support your lower back. Broaden your chest and drop your shoulders. Extend through the base of the skull toward the ceiling.

benefits stretches the lower spine ● eases aching feet ● relaxes the face ● rejuvenative for body and brain ● calms the mind

variation

■ When feeling especially in need of rest, practice with a cushion between your heels and buttocks and another one or two supporting your chest and head.

2 Exhaling, bend forward, relaxing first your navel, then your chest fully onto both thighs before letting your forehead or, if flexible, the crown of your head, come to rest lightly on the floor in front of your knees. Let your arms lie quietly beside your body, hands by your feet.

3 Focus on your breathing for 30 to 60 seconds, feeling your lower back expand with each inhalation and releasing tension with the exhalation. Let your torso melt into your thighs and make sure your buttocks remain firmly on your heels.

victory breath in perfect pose
ujjayi in siddhasana

beginner

In this session you focus on deepening your breathing and really tuning in as you make the breath audible. When you have mastered this basic breathing technique, adopt it as you hold a posture to empty your mind of other concerns and concentrate your focus while boosting will-power and releasing tension and pain. Work in Perfect Pose, a very stable and calming sitting position once you get used to the positioning of the feet. If you find it impossible, practice cross-legged until you feel more flexible. Vary the cross of the legs with each practice session.

1 Sit in Staff Pose (see page 68). Stretch your legs wide, pivot forward slightly to pull the flesh out from behind your buttocks, and sit back upright. Fold one leg in so the heel sits next to your pubic bone, the sole by the inside of the opposite thigh.

precautions

■ If you have high blood pressure, practice the breathing lying on your back.

2 Bend the other leg and draw the calf in, placing the foot on top of the lower foot, ankles and heels stacked. Rest your hands on your knees, palms upward, fingers relaxed, and lengthen up out of your pelvis. Close your eyes and focus on your breathing.

3 When you feel relaxed, inhale through both nostrils, imagining the breath dropping to your abdomen, as if inflating a balloon. Feel your diaphragm sink, your abdomen expand, and your ribcage widen at the front and back.

4 Start to exhale, contracting your throat as if humming, and expel the air gradually from the top down, feeling a whispering "haaaa" sound in your throat. This is one breath cycle. Take a regular breath, if required.

5 Repeat for up to three minutes, keeping the breathing cycles smooth, steady, and rhythmic, and allowing each in breath to come naturally. When you have been practicing for some weeks and are comfortable with the "haaaa" sound on the exhalation, start to feel it on the inhalation, too.

benefits perfect pose rests the body while keeping the mind alert, combats stiffness in the knees and ankles, and tones the lower back and abdomen • victory breath builds stamina, soothes the nerves, cleanses the body, and boosts digestion

body-awareness technique
in corpse pose savasana

While you sink into the oblivion of the Corpse Pose after this session, use this technique to help you feel the lightness of your completely relaxed body and start to sense that you are not defined solely by your physical shape and form. Work for 5 to 10 minutes.

1 Lie on your back, legs hip-width apart and extending away from you, feet and knees dropping outward. Relax your arms away from your sides so that both shoulderblades are flat to the floor. Place your palms up and loosely open. Lift your head only, look toward your toes to align it with your body, then replace on the mat, chin tucked in slightly to extend the back of the neck. Close your eyes.

precautions

■ If you are pregnant or have a respiratory disorder, raise your chest by placing a cushion beneath it; if you have lower back problems, keep your knees bent, feet flat on the floor.

2 Use the muscle-relaxation technique on pages 36–37 to tense and relax every part of the body, starting at the toes and working up to the scalp. Then scan your body for residual tension and command it to release. Allow your body to sink into the firm support of the floor.

3 When you feel relaxed and heavy, bring your focus to your breathing. Watch your regular breath move in and out for a while, witnessing the out breaths lengthen and pauses creeping in as you become more relaxed.

4 Feel how each part of your body is a dead weight sinking heavily into the floor, and yet at the same time feels completely weightless. Start at your feet. Sense how anchored they are by complete relaxation to the floor. Then notice how they tingle with lightness.

5 Repeat the exercise, working up each part of the body in turn. Feel the weight of the large muscles—the thighs, buttocks—and of the chest. Simultaneously imagine that these body parts have dissolved so you can no longer tell where you end and the room begins. Feel released from the body, and know that you are more than the sum of your physical parts.

6 Resolve to take this experience into your postures. In a pose, feel the solidity and rootedness of your body, but sense also a lightness invigorating you. Connect this to the fact that to hold a pose you need to engage a muscle by tensing it while simultaneously relaxing the opposing muscle to stretch. Ponder the notion of relaxed tension that you strive for in your yoga practice.

7 Wriggle your fingers and toes as you start to come to. Stretch, bend your knees, and roll to your right before sitting up. When you open your eyes, try to retain the sensation of vitality and well-being that you felt during the exercise.

benefits relaxes and lightens the body • regulates blood pressure • relieves stress • develops concentration • promotes feelings of inner peace

twisting and stretching to the side

upstretched hand pose
urdhva hastasana

For this warm-up exercise start standing upright with legs hip-width apart, knees slightly bent, and arms loose by your side. Keeping your hips even and relaxed, twist gently from side to side to begin the mobilization and get your heart and lungs working. Then follow the joint warm-up from Chapter 3 (see pages 40–43). Finally, begin to co-ordinate your breathing with your body movements using this side-extension exercise, which lengthens both sides of the body and boosts your strength.

1 Stand in Mountain Pose (see pages 44–45).

2 Inhaling, raise your arms overhead, bringing your forearms toward each other and palms to touch. Interlock your fingers then release any tension in your neck by dropping your shoulders toward your hips. Hold for a few breaths.

3 Exhaling, extend your spine out of your pelvis, then stretch to the left, arms still extending, body and arms on one plane. Hold for up to 30 seconds, feeling your right side lengthening and engaging the muscles on your left side to support the bend and prevent the left side from collapsing. Inhale back to center.

4 Repeat the extension up and over to the right. Exhale as you take the arms down. Unclasp your fingers and interlock them again so the opposite thumb is on top, then repeat.

revolved head to knee pose
parivrtta janu sirsasana

beginner

By revolving the trunk, too, this pose intensifies the sideways stretch begun in the warm-up. Make sure you have warmed up well before you start the poses—you might like to follow the Sun Salutation sequence before you start (see pages 124–7).

1 Sit in Staff Pose (see page 68). Stretch your legs wide, and pivot forward slightly to pull the flesh out from behind your buttocks, then extend upright, stretching out of the pelvis.

2 Fold your right leg, heel next to your pubic bone, sole against the inside of the left thigh. Press out through your left heel, knee facing the ceiling. Rest your left hand on your left leg and make sure your hips and chest face square to the front. Fold your right arm behind your lower back (grasp the top of your left thigh if possible) and, inhaling, open your chest.

3 Exhaling, lengthen your right side up and over, taking your left side toward your left thigh and reaching out, if possible, to catch your outstretched toes with your left hand. Use your left hand as a lever to help bring your left side toward your leg. Turn to look over your right shoulder.

4 Relax into the pose for 30 to 60 seconds, keeping your trunk opening up and out with each inhalation and releasing your left side toward your outstretched thigh with the exhalation. Inhale back to center, extend the bent leg, come back into Staff Pose, and repeat to the other side.

benefits tones the abdominal area
- boosts circulation to the spine
- eases backache • invigorates

barred gate pose parighasana

beginner

In this pose, the trunk again extends to the side. As you are firmly rooted on your knees, with your pelvis isolated from the movement, you might find that you can take the stretch a little further, and you will feel it more keenly.

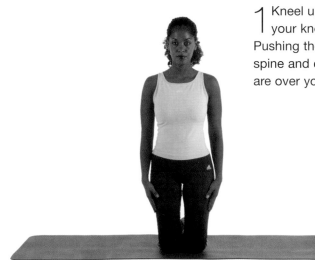

1 Kneel up with knees together, hips aligned over your knees and legs perpendicular to the floor. Pushing the pelvis forward slightly, extend the spine and open your chest so that your shoulders are over your hips.

2 Extend your left leg to the side, toes pointing away, heel down and in line with your right knee, hips facing forward. Inhaling, raise your arms to shoulder level. Stretch through your fingers to widen your chest and upper back. Release your shoulders down from your ears.

3 Exhaling, slowly take your trunk to the left, placing your left hand on your left shin and raising your right hand to the ceiling. Do not collapse the left side of the waist, and keep your whole trunk facing forward by revolving your top ribs toward the ceiling. Try not to collapse your weight onto your lower hand. Look at your raised thumb and hold, inhaling extension into both sides.

4 Exhaling, increase the sideways stretch, moving your lower hand nearer your foot, and taking your right arm over your head toward the opposite corner of the room. Try not to collapse in the waist on the bent side. Keep looking at the ceiling. Hold for up to 30 seconds. Inhale back to center, draw in your outstretched leg, and sit back on your heels for a few moments. Repeat to the other side.

benefits increases flexibility in the spine • stretches the pelvis • tones the legs • conditions the abdominal area • shapes the waist

extended side angle stretch
utthita parsvakonanasa

beginner

Similar to the last pose, this sideways extension starts from a standing position and takes the stretch through the entire side of the body, neck to ankles. It intensifies the work on your cardio-vascular system to boost the energizing effect of the sideways stretch.

1 Stand in Mountain Pose (see pages 44–45). Inhaling, jump or step your feet a little wider than 3 to 4ft (90 to 120cm) apart, outer edges parallel. Adjust your weight so it is balanced between both feet. Pull up through the inner legs. Center your pelvis, tuck your abdomen up and back, broaden your chest, and lengthen the spine up the back of your skull toward the ceiling. Extend your arms parallel to the floor, palms down.

2 Turn your left foot and thigh out 90°, your right foot in slightly. Pull your buttocks toward each other. When you feel stable, exhale and bend your left knee to make a right angle, thigh parallel to the floor. Keep your weight even between both legs and your hips forward. Lengthen from pelvis to head, continuing the line of your extended leg. Support your left side by placing your left forearm on your left thigh near your knee, fingers pointing forward. Let your right arm lie along your right side.

precautions

■ Avoid this posture if you suffer with high blood pressure.

3 Exhaling, take your right arm behind your lower back, grasping the top of your left thigh, if possible. Inhaling, open your chest toward the ceiling. Hold for a few seconds.

4 Drop your lower hand to the floor, placing your palm flat behind your foot, wrist aligned with your heel, fingers facing forward. Draw the upper arm to the ceiling. Hold briefly.

5 Stretch your upper arm over your head toward the far corner of the room to create a long stretch from your extended right ankle to your right fingertips. Look toward the ceiling and hold for up to 30 seconds. Inhaling, straighten the legs. Exhaling, take your arms to your sides and relax briefly before repeating to the other side.

variation
■ In Step 4, drop your lower hand to a block instead of the floor if you feel you can't reach.

benefits exercises the heart ● strengthens the legs ● shapes the waist and reduces fat around the hips ● opens out the chest, promoting easier deep breathing ● relieves sciatica

revolved triangle pose
parivrtta trikonasana

intermediate

Start your practice by revising the Extended Triangle Pose (see pages 48–49), then, when you feel confident, move on to this more challenging version, which by revolving the upper body through 180° tests your balance.

1 Stand in Mountain Pose (see pages 44–45). Inhaling, jump or step your feet 3 to 4ft (90 to 120cm) apart. Make sure the outer edges of your feet are parallel. Adjust your bodyweight so it is balanced between both feet. Extend up through the inner legs. Center your pelvis, tuck your abdomen up and back, broaden your chest, and lengthen the spine out of the back of your skull. Extend your arms parallel to the floor, palms face down.

2 Turn your left foot out by 90°, your right foot in by 60°. Exhaling, turn your torso to face left, making sure both hips are square and facing forward. Open your chest to bring your shoulders over your hips, and extend the spine out of the pelvis. Hold, breathing stability into your feet, legs, and hips.

precautions

■ Bend your front knee slightly if you find it difficult to balance.

variation

■ In Step 3, place your right hand on a block if you feel you can't reach to the floor.

3 Inhale, stretch your right arm up and pivot forward from the hips, placing your right hand on your left calf, ankle, or, best of all, the floor, by the inside edge of your front foot. Straighten your left arm to the ceiling to open your trunk, and look at your thumb, if possible.

4 When you have the flexibility, place your lower hand by the outside edge of your front foot. Hold for up to 30 seconds, lengthening the spine and revolving the trunk from pelvis to the crown of the head with each inhalation. With the exhalation, root down through the back leg. Come back to wide-leg standing on an inhalation. When ready, repeat to the other side.

benefits tones the thighs, hamstrings, and calves ● expands the chest ● strengthens the hips ● increases blood flow to the lower spine

torso stretch bharadvajrasana

beginner

Rotating the body from a sitting position gives you a strong, firm base from which to turn, which enables you to get deeper into the stretch as you really relax into the movement. In this simple but effective pose, the torso turns in a spiral from the hips, boosting flexibility in your back and shoulders.

1 Sit in Staff Pose (see page 68). Place your palms slightly behind your hips, fingers pointing forward. Lift out of your pelvis, extending your spine toward the ceiling.

2 Keeping your torso square, bend your knees and swivel your legs so your shins lie beside your right outer thigh, your feet next to your right hip. Ensure your thighs and knees still face forward. Place your top inside ankle into the instep of your bottom foot. Inhaling, extend upward from your buttocks.

3 Exhaling, turn your torso, from the lower abdomen up, to the left, so your right shoulder eventually aligns with your left thigh. Extend your right arm and place your hand on your left knee, using it as a lever to aid the rotation.

4 Inhale, press on your back hand and stretch up. Exhaling, rotate further, pressing down your lower shin. When you have gone as far as is comfortable, turn to look over your left shoulder and take your back arm around your waist to rest on your right thigh. Hold for 30 to 60 seconds. Come back to center on an inhalation, straighten your legs, and repeat to the other side.

benefits increases flexibility in every part of the spine • promotes suppleness in the hips • eases any lower back pain • reduces stiff shoulders and neck

precautions

■ Avoid this posture if you suffer with high blood pressure.

lateral sitting twist marichyasana

beginner

This lateral rotation works on the spine to realign it into its optimum position. The more you extend upward in the pose, the better you can turn to the side. You also experience a real grounding in your pelvis, and an invigorating massage of the abdominal organs, which boosts the feeling of being lean and clean. This stretch has the added benefit of reducing fat around the waistline. Never rush to the next stage of the movement; stay with what you can achieve comfortably, until you feel fully ready to move on.

1 Sit in Staff Pose (see page 68). Bend your left leg and place the heel near your left buttock. Stretch your right leg out, knee and toes pointing up. Hold below the left knee with both hands and extend upward, out of your pelvis. Broaden your chest and lift upward through the back of the skull.

2 Inhaling, stretch your left arm up, lengthening your side without crunching your shoulders. Feel a good extension, then place your palm behind your left hip, fingers pointing away. Lengthen upward again by pressing on this palm.

3 Catch your left leg with your right arm, and wrap your forearm below the knee. Exhaling, turn left, twisting the lower back. Keep your chest broad, and try not to collapse onto your back hand; keep lifting upward. Hold until you feel stable.

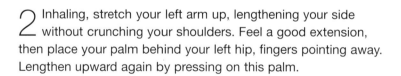

4 Keeping your back straight, hips level, and top knee upright, twist farther to the left, taking the back of your upper right arm against the outer side of your left knee and shin. Bend your arm, palm facing forward, forearm vertical, fingers pointing upward. Exhaling, turn to look as far over your left shoulder as possible. Hold for up to 30 seconds, stretching up with each inhalation, and rotating with the exhalations, using your bent leg as a lever.

5 Once you feel confident, extend the bent right arm back around your shin, palm facing outward. Take your other arm back around your waist to catch the right hand. Anchor through the left foot and increase the twist. Hold. Inhale back to center, come back into Staff Pose, then repeat to the other side.

benefits tones the abdominal area and improves digestion ● shapes the waist ● said to slow the ageing process ● eases backache ● relieves constipation ● energizes

lengthening the out breath in thunderbolt pose
khumbhaka in vajrasana

Detox your mind and body with this cleansing yoga breathing technique, which lengthens the out breath to rid the body of toxins. The addition of a pause to the breathing pattern also encourages the mind to relax completely. Sit in Thunderbolt Pose, a kneeling posture used in many meditative traditions since it grounds the body powerfully, allowing serenity and calmness to develop.

variation

■ If your legs are particularly stiff, place a cushion or block under your knees and buttocks to ease pressure on the feet, or between your ankles to cushion uncomfortably knobbly bits.

1 Kneel with feet touching, knees together, hips over knees, shoulders over hips. Sit back, pressing your buttocks on your heels to flatten your feet to the floor. Rest your hands, palms down, on your thighs. As your body weight sinks down through your pelvis, inhale space into the lower legs, and exhale away any tightness or tension.

precautions

■ If you are straining to hold your breath, reduce the count.
■ Practice in Corpse Pose if you want a deeper relaxation.
■ If you find this too difficult, do the breathing exercise from chapters 3 or 4 instead.

2 Lengthen out of your pelvis, tucking your abdomen slightly in and up to support the lower back, broadening your chest, and releasing your shoulders away from your ears. Tuck your chin in and release the back of your skull toward the ceiling. Close your eyes and focus on your breathing.

3 Inhale to a count of four. Pause, holding for a count of four without tensing or letting the shoulders rise, then exhale for four. This is one breath cycle. Take a regular breath, if necessary. Work for 2 to 3 minutes, and practice for some weeks, until it feels natural.

4 When you feel comfortable with the technique, start to lengthen the out breath. Inhale for four, pause for four, and exhale to the count of eight. Take a regular breath, if necessary. Let the in breath come naturally and easily. Work for 2 to 3 minutes, keeping the rhythm easy.

benefits thunderbolt pose tones the thighs, stretches out the top of the feet and ankles, works on the knee joints, promotes stability, and calms the mind ● lengthening the out-breath is said to enhance longevity, reduce cravings, and draw the mind into meditation

breath visualization
in corpse pose savasana

To complete this session, you adopt the Corpse Pose, as before, but work on taking the breath to various parts of the body to release tension and energize your limbs. If you feel the cold, cover yourself from shoulders to toes with a soft blanket before starting the exercise. Work for 5 to 10 minutes.

1 Lie on your back, legs hip-width apart and extending away from you, feet and knees dropping outward. Relax your arms away from your sides so that both shoulderblades are flat to the floor. Place your palms up and loosely open. Lift your head only, look toward your toes to align it with your body, then replace on the mat, chin tucked in slightly to extend the back of the neck. Close your eyes.

2 Use the muscle-relaxation technique on pages 36–37 to tense and relax every part of the body, starting at the toes and working up to the scalp. Then scan your body for residual tension and command it to release, allowing your body to sink into the firm support of the floor.

precautions

■ If you are pregnant or have a respiratory disorder, raise your chest by placing a cushion beneath it; if you have lower back problems, keep your knees bent, feet flat on the floor.

3 When you feel relaxed and heavy, start to focus on your breath. Watch your regular breath in and out for a while, then picture the breath starting at your toes and rising up your legs to ignite the energy center found in the navel region. Feel the area tingle with vitality. As you exhale, send this energy rushing back down through your legs to enliven them. Repeat a few times.

4 Next imagine the breath starting at your fingertips; as you inhale, pull the energy up your arms, around your shoulders, and down your spine to the energy reservoir at your navel center. Feel the life force enlivening your abdomen. As you exhale, let it fill your spine, shoulders, arms, and fingers with a zingy freshness. Repeat a few times.

5 Finally, breathe in energy through your fingers and toes and let it run up your spine to the crown of your head. Imagine breathing it out through the third-eye area between your eyebrows. Repeat a few times, then just relax, breathing regularly for while before wriggling your fingers and toes. Stretch, bend your knees, and roll to the right before coming to sitting. When you open your eyes, try to retain the sensation of energy and complete relaxation.

benefits relaxes and re-energizes the body • regulates blood pressure • relieves stress • develops concentration • promotes feelings of inner peace

chapter 6

backbends

● **warming up 102–105**

chest and shoulder opener

The four warm-up exercises here are adapted from six Tibetan Rites, which activate the body's energy centers. They are demanding, so start with a few repetitions—seven of each performed slowly is still effective—building up to 14 or, ideally, 21 of each, practiced at some speed. Focus on your breathing in each exercise as the strenuous movements build up a sweat and tune you out of the everyday world.

1 Sitting in Thunderbolt Pose (see pages 96–97), interlock your fingers behind your head and grab the sides of your neck with your palms, elbows facing forward. Give the back of your neck a good squeeze to massage out tension.

2 Sit up straight, extending out of your pelvis. Inhaling, open your elbows wide, stretching across the front of your chest and bringing your shoulderblades together. Hold as you complete the in breath.

3 Exhaling, bring your elbows together, dropping your chin to compress your throat, and feeling a good stretch across your upper back. Let the breath draw your abdomen in and back. This is one cycle. Repeat the cycle up to 21 times; start with 7 if you are a complete beginner.

leg and neck raise

1 Lie on your back, legs extended and arms by your side, palms down. Align your head with your body in a Full Body Stretch.

2 Inhaling, raise both legs simultaneously until perpendicular to the floor, knees straight. At the same time, without raising your shoulders, lift your neck. Hold until you complete the inhalation. If this feels too strenuous, or you have lower back problems, raise each leg alternately and bend the other leg, placing the foot on the floor.

3 Exhaling, lower your legs and head with control to the floor. Relax briefly. This is one cycle. Repeat the cycle up to 21 times; work toward 7 times if you are a beginner.

throat and chest stretch

1 Sit in Staff Pose (see page 68), palms by your hips, fingers facing forward. Take your legs hip-width apart and bend your knees, soles of the feet to the floor.

2 Inhaling, press on your palms and feet to raise your torso to the ceiling, creating a table-top shape from hips to shoulders. Drop your head back to look behind.

3 Exhaling, drop your hips down and back between your palms, taking your chin to your chest to compress your throat as you complete the exhalation. This is one cycle. Repeat the cycle up to 21 times; start with 7 if you are new to yoga.

downward to upward dog

1 Start on hands and knees, legs
hip-width apart. Turn your toes
under. Exhaling, lift your hips high
and press back with your arms into
Downward Facing Dog Pose (see
pages 64–65). Relax your neck and
head as you hold briefly.

2 Inhaling, press forward on your palms, bend your elbows,
and in one flowing action take your head, shoulders, and
hips forward and down. Still inhaling and keeping the movement
fluid, press on your palms to arch the upper body into Upward
Facing Dog Pose (see pages 66–67). This is one cycle. Exhaling,
press on your hands to take the hips back up into Downward
Dog as you repeat the cycle, switching between the two poses
fluidly. Start with one repetition, building up to the maximum
number (21) as you gain in strength.

3 Drop your hips back onto your heels and rest in Child
Pose (see pages 74–75) for a few minutes.

standing forward bend uttanasana

intermediate

It may seem strange to start bending backward by bending forward, but this pose is important to give an intense stretch to the lower back and back of the legs, and to increase flexibility in the hips. This allows the pelvis to turn over the thigh bones, permitting more effective backbending. The pose is valuable at the start of a yoga session to slow the body (it decreases the heart rate), relaxing it in preparation for the challenging stretches to come.

1 Stand in Mountain Pose (see pages 44–45). Inhaling, extend your arms overhead, bringing your forearms toward each other and releasing any tension in your neck by dropping your shoulders away from your ears. Look up if desired. Hold for a couple of breath cycles.

2 Exhaling, hinge forward from the hips, keeping your head lifted. If you are flexible, take your fingertips or palms to the ground as shown. If not, work with bent knees.

3 Check that your weight is not too far
back. If it is, move your hips forward
until your bodyweight descends through
the balls of your feet and your buttocks
extend toward the ceiling. Relax your
head and neck downward.

4 Relax into the pose for 30 to 60 seconds. Keeping your feet
active, imagine drawing each breath up the back of your
legs, then down your spine. Let gravity release the back of the
legs, lengthen the spine away from the hips, and take the head
down. Work to straighten the legs as you exhale.

5 Finally, when you have achieved a good level of
flexibility, stretch your hands to rest behind your
legs, catching one wrist with the other hand. Bring
your abdomen, chest, and then your face to meet
your legs. On an inhalation, come back up to
standing as you went down, head last.

benefits revives body and mind
• rejuvenates the spine • slows the
heart rate • promotes detoxification
by stimulating the kidneys and liver
• relieves sciatica • eases stomach
ache • relaxes the brain

precautions

■ If you have disc problems, work only
to step 2.

crescent moon pose anjaneyasana

intermediate

With this stretch, you warm up and extend the psoas muscle, the hip flexor, which rarely gets a full stretch in everyday life but plays a vital role in backbending. When this muscle is tight, the lower back feels a pull because it cannot stretch but when it is flexible, you can stretch up and out of the lower back.

1 Sit in Thunderbolt Pose (see pages 96–97). Kneel up, hips directly over your knees, and extend your spine from its base to the crown of your head.

2 Inhaling, take a good step forward with your right foot, then center your knee over your ankle to create a right angle with the floor, shin vertical. Rest your palms on your front knee.

3 Exhaling, push your trunk and front thigh forward without moving the foot, so your back leg stretches into a lunge. Drop your pelvis and feel the stretch in your left front thigh. Hold for a few breath cycles, stabilizing the upper body over the front heel.

4 Inhaling, stretch your arms forward and up, extending out of the hips equally on both sides, broadening your chest, and releasing the shoulders downward. Do not compress the lower spine. Hold for a few breath cycles.

5 If desired, inhale, stretch up again, then arch the upper back gently backward. Open the chest and carefully take the head back, chin pointing to the ceiling. Hold for 10 to 20 seconds. Inhale to come up, sit back in Thunderbolt Pose, then repeat on the other side.

benefits tones the legs ● strengthens the ankles ● works on the abdominal area ● opens the chest to promote deep breathing

precautions

■ If you feel pressure in the lower back, work only to step 3.

half locust pose ardha salabhasana

intermediate

A strengthening stretch, Locust Pose works on the lower spine, pelvis, and hamstrings to prepare them for supporting the spine during backbends. To get the most out of the stretch, make sure to stretch your legs and torso well before starting to lift. This relieves pressure on the lower back and opens the pelvis. This pose gives the intestines, kidneys, liver, and pancreas a workout, which can leave you feeling light and cleansed. It also boosts circulation for an allover kick. Don't progress to the final position until you feel really strong and confident.

1 Lie on your front, legs outstretched and touching, arms by your sides, palms facing up, chin on the floor. Make sure your chest and shoulders are square and opening down into the floor.

2 On an exhalation, firmly stretch your left leg away, pointing your toes at the wall behind you.

3 Imagining your left thigh is heavy and keeping the whole leg straight, inhale, raising your calf and thigh as if trying to place your sole on the ceiling. Isolate the stretch in the buttock and keep the spine relaxed. Hold for a few breath cycles, then lower on an exhalation. Repeat on the other leg.

4 When you are comfortable in the pose, make your hands into fists and place them beneath your hips, arms straight, palms up. Exhaling, stretch both legs away from your spine, thighs and calves touching, feet together. Then, imagining your thighs are heavy, inhale and raise both legs, as if trying to place your soles on the ceiling. Work to lift your pelvis away from your fists. Keep your shoulders opening into the floor and your chin anchored. Hold for 20 to 30 seconds. Exhale back to the prone position. Push your buttocks back onto your heels and rest in Child Pose (see pages 74–75).

benefits strengthens the hamstrings • eases lower backache • boosts digestion • promotes stamina • said to increase youthfulness

precautions

■ If you have lower back problems, practice with bent legs and knees apart, working to bring the knees up and together.

cobra pose bhujangasana

advancing beginner

Now you have prepared the lower back for backbending, work on the upper back, shoulders, and chest. In this pose, focus on your chest broadening and lifting and your shoulders dropping back, rather than thinking about bending your spine.

1 Lie prone, forehead on the ground and legs outstretched and touching. Plant your hands beneath your shoulders, fixing both palms and fingers to the ground, fingertips in line with the top of your shoulders, little fingers with the edge of your shoulders. Tuck your elbows toward your waist. Exhaling, extend your legs back and your spine forward, lengthening the lower back.

precautions

■ If you have lower back problems, work only to step 2.

benefits tones the spine ● opens the chest ● boosts digestion ● beneficial for asthma ● eases menstrual disorders ● relieves insomnia

2 Inhaling, lengthen your upper body forward, then lift your torso. Do not press too much on the palms, and do not compress the lower back. Instead, focus on lengthening the upper spine forward, opening your chest, and dropping your shoulders. It helps to draw back through your elbows. Point your chin forward and up, keeping your neck long. Hold for 20 to 30 seconds.

3 Once you become more flexible, straighten the arms to gain an even stretch along each part of the spine. Exhaling, unroll down slowly. Push your buttocks back onto your heels and rest in Child Pose (see pages 74–75).

bow pose dhanurasana

intermediate

It's now time to involve the whole back in the stretch. This strong pose strengthens every part of the back, and works the pelvis and thighs, too, promoting great stamina. As you work, take your attention to every vertebra, making sure to feel the stretch around each one.

1 Lie on your front, forehead on the ground and legs outstretched. Rest your arms by your sides, palms up. Exhaling, lengthen your legs away from your lower back and open your chest and shoulders down into the floor.

precautions

■ If you have lower back problems, work only to step 2.

2 Inhaling, bend your legs at the knees and press the front of your pelvis into the mat. On the next exhalation, stretch your arms back and grab your ankles.

3 Keeping your hips and groin pressing down, inhale and pull on your ankles to raise your chest, simultaneously lifting your legs up and away so the thighs rise. Let your legs extend your arms, and allow the pulling of the arms to open your chest. Look forward and up, and draw your shoulders back and your upper spine in. Hold for up to 20 seconds, extending the front of the body and front of the thighs equally so the shoulders and knees are level.

4 Lower carefully to the floor on an exhalation and release each leg. Lie prone for a few seconds. Push your buttocks back onto your heels and rest in Child Pose (see pages 74–75).

benefits increases spinal flexibility • combats hunched shoulders • regarded as one of the best postures to ease digestive disorders • regulates the menstrual cycle • massages the heart, liver, pancreas, and kidneys • regulates the endocrine glands

intense back stretch paschimottanasana

End your backbending as you started it, by relaxing forward and letting gravity take over to lengthen the spine and back of the legs worked by the previous postures. Forward bending after backbending can also ease feelings of dizziness or over-exertion as the brain and body rest, and the mind and senses are allowed space to replenish. Work gradually, and never force the stretch, especially after backbends. You may like to practice the twists in Chapter 5 again after this pose: gentle twists are an excellent way to release the spine after a strenuous workout.

1 Sit in Staff Pose (see page 68). Sit upright, lifting up from the lower back, and squaring your shoulders over your hips. Feel the crown of your head lifting toward the ceiling. Inhaling, extend your arms overhead, growing taller without tensing your shoulders.

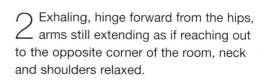

2 Exhaling, hinge forward from the hips, arms still extending as if reaching out to the opposite corner of the room, neck and shoulders relaxed.

3 Drop your hands to your calves, ankles, or toes, and open the chest as you pivot forward and down with each exhalation. Do not round your back. Exhaling, relax both thighs to the floor and push out through the edges of your feet. If you wish, place a bolster on your thighs and recline onto it.

4 With each exhalation, extend a little further forward, until your abdomen, chest, and finally your forehead come to rest on your thighs, kneecaps, and shins.

5 If you are flexible, place your hands beyond your feet (grasp your wrist with your other fingers). Rest here for 30 to 60 seconds, keeping the navel moving forward with each out breath, and breathing into any tension at the back of the legs. Inhale back to Staff Pose.

benefits slows the heart rate
• boosts digestion • energizes
• enhances kidney, pancreas, and bladder function • relieves fatigue
• calms the brain

alternate nostril breathing in half lotus pose

anuloma viloma in ardha padmasana

For this breathing exercise, you sit in a preparatory position for Lotus Pose, the traditional posture of meditation. Each time you work, swap legs so you don't start to favor one side. The hands are worked, too, with *mudra* hand gestures, which activate energy points on the palms and fingers rather like an acupressure self-massage. The breathing exercise alternates between the nostrils, which stimulates powerful energy channels in the body to relax and revive you.

1 Sit in Staff Pose (see page 68). Spread your legs wide, then bend your left leg, bringing the foot toward the right thigh so the heel abuts the pubic bone and the sole presses against the top of the right inner thigh.

2 Bend your right leg and, supporting the right foot from beneath with both hands, bring it over to rest on your left thigh, outer edge by the groin, sole facing upward. Inhaling, lengthen your spine taking the crown of the head toward the ceiling. Watch your breathing become calm and slower for a few moments.

precautions

■ Avoid if you have high blood pressure or heart problems.

3 Fold the first and middle fingers on your right hand into your palm. Take your hand to your nose. Rest your ring and little fingers on your left nostril, your thumb on your right nostril. Place your left hand, palm upward, on your left knee, thumb and first finger lightly joined.

4 Close your eyes. Inhale through both nostrils, block your left nostril with the ring and little fingers, and exhale through your right nostril. Inhale active energy through your right nostril.

5 At the top of the inhalation, block your right nostril with your thumb, and exhale through your left nostril. Inhale through your left nostril. This is one cycle. Repeat up to 7 cycles, building up to 3 minutes. Finish on an exhalation from the right nostril, then inhale through both nostrils. Exhale as you uncurl your legs.

benefits Half Lotus relaxes the body while keeping the mind alert, eases stiff knees and ankles, and tones the spine and abdominal area • Alternate Nostril Breathing cleanses the body, calms the mind, boosts concentration, and harmonizes energy levels

light visualization
in corpse pose savasana

As usual, relax in the Corpse Pose to complete your yoga practice, giving time for your body to adjust to the stretches you have just performed. Explore the following visualization, or, if you prefer, just stick to one of the simple techniques of previous sessions—choose whichever appeals to you most. Work for 5 to 10 minutes.

1 Lie on your back, legs hip-width apart and extending away from you, feet and knees dropping outward. Relax your arms away from your sides so that both shoulderblades are flat to the floor. Place your palms up and loosely open. Lift your head only, look toward your toes to align it with your body, then replace on the mat, chin tucked in slightly to extend the back of the neck. Close your eyes.

2 Use the muscle-relaxation technique on pages 36–37 to tense and relax every part of the body, starting at the toes and working up to the scalp. Then scan your body for residual tension and command it to release. Allow your body to sink into the firm support of the floor.

3 When you feel relaxed and heavy, bring your focus to your breathing. Watch your regular breath move in and out for a while, witnessing the out breaths lengthen and pauses creeping in as you become more relaxed.

4 Imagine a ball of white light spinning above the crown of your head. As you inhale, picture the light energizing your brain. Then imagine the ball of light moving to the third-eye area between your eyebrows. Breathe in its energy.

5 When you feel ready, imagine the ball of light-releasing tension in your throat area and bringing new energy to this region. Then let the light ignite your heart region; breathe in vitality as you visualize the light lighting you up.

6 Take the ball of light to your solar-plexus area, and again picture it filling you with brightness. Finally, let the light enliven the area around your navel and then your pelvis dissolving tension and infusing you with a sense of well-being.

7 Take a few minutes to bathe in the sensation of light before wriggling your fingers and toes as you start to come to. Stretch, bend your knees, and roll to your right side before sitting up. When you open your eyes, try to retain the sensation of vitality and well-being that you felt during the relaxation.

benefits relaxes the body ● energizes ● regulates blood pressure ● relieves stress ● develops concentration ● promotes feelings of inner peace

chapter 7

introducing inversions

sun salutation surya namaskar

Follow the basic joint mobilization exercises on pages 40–43, then warm up the body with this Sun Salutation sequence. Start slowly, working to perfect each pose, and build up to 7 repetitions on each side, co-ordinating your breathing with the movements. Traditionally, this sequence is performed facing East to greet the rising sun.

1 Stand in Mountain Pose (see pages 44–45). When you feel calm and stable, bring your palms and fingers together in prayer position in front of your chest, pressing your thumbs into your sternum to activate the heart energy center.

2 Inhaling, extend your arms overhead, shoulders relaxed, arms covering the ears. Then take the stretch backward, separating the arms slightly, and look behind.

3 Exhaling, pivot forward from the hips into Standing Forward Bend (see pages 106–107). Plant your palms on either side of your feet and relax your head; focus on straightening the legs without letting the spine curve.

4 On the next inhalation, take the right leg back into a lunge position, knee slightly raised, left heel remaining flat to the floor and left knee upward. Raise your chest and look up.

5 Retaining the breath, take the front leg back and hold yourself on hands and feet like an angled plank in a press-up position. Lock the arms and relax the shoulders, taking your bodyweight in your upper arms. Look slightly forward. Don't let the hips drop.

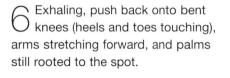

6 Exhaling, push back onto bent knees (heels and toes touching), arms stretching forward, and palms still rooted to the spot.

7 On an inhalation, press forward, take your buttocks in the air, leaving your knees, feet, and palms in contact with the floor. Lightly touch your nose and forehead to the floor.

8 On the same inhalation, press on your hands and back into your elbow creases to bring the chest forward and up into Cobra Pose (see pages 112–13). Extend the back of your neck, and look up. Tuck your elbows toward your waist. Relax your shoulders and try not to compress the lower back.

9 With the next exhalation, push your hips upward and lengthen out of the shoulders into Downward Facing Dog Pose (see pages 64–65). Work to press your heels down.

10 Inhale and step your right leg forward, back into the lunge pose and look up again, as in step 4.

11 Exhaling, bring your back leg forward and push your sitting bones upward, working to straighten the knees, as in step 3.

12 Inhaling, draw your hands in prayer position up your body and overhead. Open your arms and extend backward, as in step 2.

13 Exhaling, bring your hands back into prayer position in front of your chest, bringing chin to chest to bow your head to the sun.

14 Repeat the steps, but taking back and forward the left leg in steps 4 and 10. This is one cycle. Work up to a repetition of seven cycles.

upright extended foot pose
urdhva prasarita padasana

beginner

As well as lengthening the hamstrings, leg raises work to strengthen the abdominal muscles, which need to be kept active to support the spine as it extends upward in the inversion poses. If you have lower back problems, or don't yet have the strength to raise both legs together, stay with the single leg raises until you feel more confident in the pose.

1 Lie on your back with legs together, arms relaxed by your side, palms down. Flex your feet. Tip your pelvis forward slightly to remove any arching from the lower back.

2 Inhaling, lift your left leg, pressing out through the heel until it points toward the ceiling. Keep the right leg stretched out, extending into the heel. Hold for 30 to 60 seconds. Work to straighten the leg. Keep your lower back and pelvis heavy on the floor, your shoulders relaxed, and your neck long.

precautions

■ If you have lower back problems, work with one leg only, keeping the other leg bent, foot flat to the floor.

3 Exhale as, keeping your leg straight, you lower it to the floor with control, then relax your abdominal and leg muscles briefly, allowing the foot to drop outward. Repeat, raising the other leg, then repeat again on each side.

4 When you are happy with the single leg lifts and can straighten the legs, inhale and lift both legs with control to 90°, pressing out through the heels. Hold for 30 to 60 seconds, pressing out through both sides of each foot and heel. Feel the width of your sitting bones against the floor and the length of your spine, especially in your lower back and the back of your neck, firm against the floor.

benefits tones the abdominal muscles • strengthens the lower back • builds the leg muscles • relieves gastro-intestinal problems

5 Lower straight legs with control on an exhalation, then relax your abdominal and leg muscles briefly, allowing both feet to drop outward. Repeat twice more, then pull your knees toward your chest and, exhaling, press them into your abdomen.

supine twist jathara parivartanasana

beginner

Keeping the body in the same position—lying on your back—use a lateral twist to increase the flexibility of the spine and the shoulders in preparation for inverting the body. This pose also helps to relieve an aching back.

1 Still lying on your back, bend your knees and bring your soles to the floor. Spread your arms out in line with your shoulders, keeping the shoulders and the back of the hands flat to the mat.

2 Roll to your left side, stacking your knees and ankles, and placing your right palm on your left palm. Turn your head to gaze along your arms.

3 Inhaling, lift your right arm to the ceiling; exhaling, return it to its original position on the floor.

4 Turn your head to look along your right arm. Hold for 30 to 60 seconds, knees and ankles stacked, top hip directly over bottom hip, and resting on the floor. Inhale into areas of stiffness in the lower back, and into the shoulders and armpits to encourage them to drop toward the floor. With each exhalation, try to ease both shoulders nearer the floor.

benefits boosts flexibility in the spine and hips • reduces fat around the abdomen • tones the liver, spleen, and pancreas • relieves abdominal complaints and backache

5 Inhaling, bring the right arm back to join the left and exhaling, roll back to center to lie on your back. Repeat to the other side.

bridge pose setu bandha sarvangasana

beginner

Work the buttocks with this partial inversion. Don't go any further with the inversion poses until you feel at ease in this posture. Your throat receives a good massage from being pressed into the chest with this pose; this can seem odd at first, but go with it, breathing smoothly, and relaxing the facial muscles as it is very rejuvenative and good for stimulating the thyroid gland. Enjoy also the expansion in the chest.

1 Lie on your back, arms by your sides, palms down. Bend your knees, and place your feet, hip-width apart, close to your buttocks. Make sure the outside edges of your feet are parallel. Feel the entire length of your back, from the base of the spine to the back of the neck, dropping toward the floor.

2 Inhaling, contract your buttocks and raise your hips, pressing down on the back of your arms and tops of your shoulders. Don't take the strain in the back of your waist; tuck your abdomen in and up.

3 If desired, interlock your fingers and stretch your arms away along the floor. Hold for 30 to 60 seconds, keeping the hips and thighs lifting, squeezing the thighs toward each other, and grounding down through your heels. With each inhalation open your chest, pressing down through your shoulders. Let your throat get a good compression.

4 To come down, exhale as you lower your spine to the floor with control, vertebra by vertebra. Bring your knees to your chest and relax for a few moments.

benefits firms the buttocks • boosts flexibility in the spine • expands the chest, promoting easier deep breathing • reduces neck strain • rests the brain • eases insomnia

shoulderstand sarvangasana

intermediate

This queen of yoga postures suffuses the brain and upper body, including vital glands, with a good flow of oxygenated blood, which leaves you feeling revitalized, yet calm and completely relaxed. Don't push yourself to achieve the final position all at once. Get the foundation right over some weeks and your practice will move more speedily.

precautions

■ Do not practice during menstruation or if you have high blood pressure; work with an experienced yoga teacher if you have neck problems.

1 Lie on your back, legs outstretched, arms by your side, palms down. Bend your knees and place your feet flat on the floor. Take a few moments to feel every part of the spine from your lower back to the back of your neck dropping toward the floor. Feel your pelvis widen and soften against the mat; let your shoulders move toward your hips. Relax the backs of the arms.

2 Exhaling, press your arms into the floor and lift your legs, bringing them over your chest and toward your head.

3 Place your hands on your lower back on either side of the spine, fingers pointing up. Exhaling again, press on your arms and take your body up until your legs are at a 45° angle to the floor. Stay in this Half Shoulderstand position until you feel confident, drawing your elbows toward each other and pressing the upper arms down.

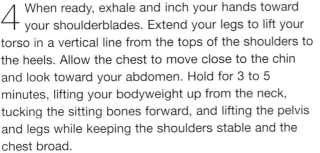

4 When ready, exhale and inch your hands toward your shoulderblades. Extend your legs to lift your torso in a vertical line from the tops of the shoulders to the heels. Allow the chest to move close to the chin and look toward your abdomen. Hold for 3 to 5 minutes, lifting your bodyweight up from the neck, tucking the sitting bones forward, and lifting the pelvis and legs while keeping the shoulders stable and the chest broad.

5 Progress to Plow Pose (see pages 136–37) or, exhaling, lower your back vertebra by vertebra, bending your legs and using your outstretched arms, palms down, like brakes. Extend your legs and let your feet drop outward, or pull your knees toward your chest to relax for a few minutes.

benefits reduces high blood pressure • stimulates every internal organ • boosts digestion • massages the thyroid and parathyroid glands • balances hormone production • boosts skin tone • relieves varicose veins • eases asthma symptoms • relieves sore throat, sinus problems, headaches • eases constipation • antidote to insomnia • detoxes • energizes • calms the brain • increases confidence

plow pose halasana

intermediate

Begin this posture from the end of step 4 of the Shoulderstand (see page 135). This is a profoundly relaxing posture and you may find you can hold it more easily than you had imagined. If you feel any strain in your throat or face, come out of the pose, relax for a few minutes, then start again, consciously relaxing your eyes, ears, face, and throat.

1 From Shoulderstand, on an exhalation, lower your extended legs to the floor behind your head. Keep the spine extending from the back of the neck to the pelvis, and rest your feet on tiptoes,

precautions

■ Do not practice during menstruation or if you have high blood pressure; work with an experienced yoga teacher if you have neck problems.

benefits creates mobility in the spine and shoulders ● expands the chest ● rejuvenates the complexion ● regulates blood pressure ● boosts the digestive system ● massages the thyroid and parathyroid glands ● relieves insomnia ● energizes ● calms the mind

2 Stretch your arms along the floor behind you, interlocking your fingers if desired. Fix your gaze on your navel, and feel each inhalation deep in the abdomen. Hold for 3 minutes or longer, keeping the spine lifting.

3 To come out of the pose, exhale and curl your back down vertebra by vertebra, bending your legs and using your outstretched arms like brakes. Stop if necessary, take an in breath, and continue your descent on the out breath. Extend your legs and let your feet drop outward or pull your knees toward your chest to relax for a few minutes.

fish pose matsyasana

beginner

Don't neglect this pose; it is the counterpose to the Shoulderstand (see page 134), easing out the neck in the opposite direction and opening the chest and throat after the inversion. This pose brings you back into balance—some teachers describe it as coming into neutral—ready for the final Corpse Pose. When you hold this pose for some minutes, the sense of peace you experience when relaxing into the Corpse Pose can be overwhelming.

1 Lie on your back, legs outstretched and together, arms by your side, palms down. Slide each palm beneath your pelvis, buttocks resting on the back of the hands.

2 Inhaling, press down through your elbows to lengthen your abdomen and upper spine, lifting your chest. Extend through your upper arms and shoulders to open your chest to the ceiling. Do not compress your lower back.

3 Carefully lift your chin forward and up, lengthening the neck. Roll your shoulders back and, keeping the lift in the upper back and chest, take your head back to rest on the crown of the head. Look backward, eyes open wide. Keep your legs active but relaxing downward. Hold for 30 seconds or longer. Relax down on an exhalation.

benefits increases mobility in the pelvis • relieves tense neck and shoulders • expands the chest for easier breathing • works the thyroid and parathyroid glands

skull shining in hero pose
kapalabhati in virasana

This cleansing technique completes your yoga session, offering a chance to rid yourself of the toxins that the poses have stimulated the body to give up. The technique removes excess carbon dioxide and brings in fresh air to revitalize every part of the body and make the brain sparkle. In some yoga circles, it is known as skull-shining for the stimulating effect it has on the inner part of the skull. The sitting pose takes the kneeling Thunderbolt Pose (see pages 96–97) a little further.

precautions

■ Avoid this breathing technique if you suffer with high blood pressure.

1 Kneel with knees, heels, and toes touching. Kneel up aligning your shoulders, hips, and knees, toes pointing directly behind you. Sit back, easing your calves to the side so your buttocks drop between them and rest on the floor. Make sure the outer thighs and calves touch. Rest your palms on your knees.

variation

■ If your sitting bones don't reach the floor, support them by placing a cushion or block between your legs.

2 Inhale space into the legs and knees, and extend up and out of the pelvis. Exhale out any tightness or tension, tucking your abdomen slightly in and up to reduce the curve in the lower back. Feel the weight of your body in contact with the ground as the crown of your head lengthens toward the ceiling. Broaden your chest and drop your shoulders away from your ears. Close your eyes and focus on your breathing.

3 When you are ready, take a long, full breath in through your nostrils. Imagine it dropping into the lower part of your abdomen, as if filling a balloon from the bottom up.

benefits Hero Pose helps counter flat feet, eases abdominal heaviness, develops will-power and strength, and boosts immunity ● Skull Shining detoxes, tones the abdominal muscles, exhilarates, and is said to reduce wrinkles

4 With your mouth closed, expel the inhalation by pulling your navel toward your spine sharply three or more times. Feel stale air leaving the body, cleansing on its way the back of your throat and the top of the palate. Relax your abdomen to let the in breath come naturally and smoothly. This is one breath. Repeat 3 cycles of 10 breaths, returning to regular breathing between each round.

loving-kindness meditation in corpse pose metta bhvana in savasana

As ever, the Corpse Pose completes your yoga practice. To end this session, try a powerful meditation technique from the Buddhist tradition that sends out love to the world. This may sound trite, but when practiced in good faith, metta bhvana can leave even the most cynical person in tears. Have a go, and feel your yoga extend as you try to take some love out of your practice and into the world. Work for 5 to 10 minutes.

1 Lie on your back, legs hip-width apart and extending away from you, feet and knees dropping outward. Relax your arms away from your sides so that both shoulderblades are flat to the floor. Place your palms up and loosely open. Lift your head only, look toward your toes to align it with your body, then replace on the mat, chin tucked in slightly to extend the back of the neck. Close your eyes.

precautions

■ If you are pregnant or have a respiratory disorder, raise your chest by placing a cushion beneath it; if you have lower back problems, keep your knees bent, feet flat on the floor.

2 Use the muscle-relaxation technique on pages 36–37 to tense and relax every part of the body, starting at the toes and working up to the scalp. Then scan your body for residual tension and command it to release. Allow your body to sink into the firm support of the floor.

3 When you feel relaxed and heavy, bring your focus to your breathing. Watch your regular breath move in and out for a while, witnessing the out breaths lengthen and pauses creeping in as you become more relaxed.

4 Start to contemplate a time when you felt perfectly happy, secure, and at peace. Try not to get caught up in the details, just let the sensation flood you. Repeat the phrase, "May I be perfectly happy" to yourself, meaning it.

5 Think about someone who has given you love—maybe a parent, partner, or child. Let the feeling of love and security you conjured up in step 4 fill your heart. Send it out to that person, saying, "May he/she be perfectly happy."

6 When you feel ready, call up those same feelings again; this time, extend them to someone you like, but don't love, maybe a friend or workmate. Repeat the phrase "May he/she be perfectly happy." Feel that it envelops the recipient with feelings of security and love.

7 Now extend the intent toward someone you don't know well, perhaps a neighbor, bus driver, or coffeeshop worker. Use the same phrase.

benefits relaxes the body
• regulates blood pressure
• relieves stress • develops concentration • promotes inner peace • develops compassion

8 Let that love fill you again, then send it without thinking too much to someone you dislike. Don't engage too much if it's painful. Include yourself, too, if it helps, saying, "May we be perfectly happy." Do this even if you don't mean it. Finally, extend your love unconditionally to all living things, repeating the phrase one last time.

9 Lie quietly for a while. If this has stirred up difficult emotions, give yourself time to readjust. Then wriggle your fingers and toes, stretch, bend your knees, and roll to your right side to rest before sitting up.

chapter 8
programs

- rise and shine sequence
- bedtime sequence
- women only sequence
- energizing sequence
- relaxing sequence
- yoga at your desk
- yoga in the car

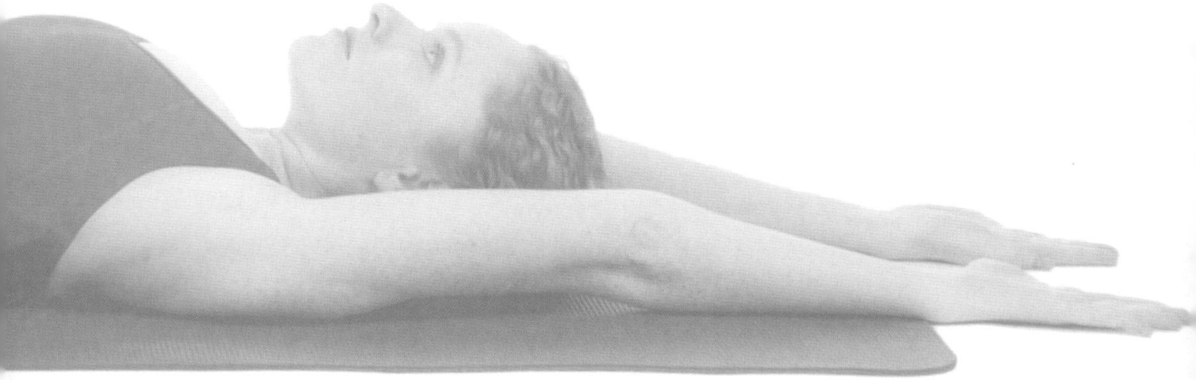

rise and shine sequence

The most effective yoga is done in the early morning just after waking. Your energy levels are most responsive at this time, and the practice sets up your body and mind to be well balanced and respond positively to every experience the day throws at you.

10 minutes

Full body stretch: while still in bed with eyes closed, stretch first your legs, then your arms, then both simultaneously to their full extent.

Corpse pose with legs bent: bend your knees and place your feet on the mattress. Gently cover your eye sockets (with no pressure) using the fleshy part of your palms. Open your eyes and look into the darkness of your palms. Then gently massage your face, sweeping around your jawline from chin to temples, along the cheekbones from sides of nose to temples, and from center of the forehead to temples. Press at the temples each time to activate the energy point here.

Supine twist: still lying in bed, stretch your arms out and take your bent legs to the side.

Cat pose: get out of bed, bringing your head up last, then let this pose wake up every part of the spine.

Child pose: sink back on your knees and watch your breath as the inhalations lift the back of your rib cage.

Mountain pose: come to standing and align your body. Take some good, deep inhalations, and exhale fully.

Upstretched hand pose: feel an enlivening stretch on both sides.

Standing wheel pose: open the chest to promote deep breathing.

Standing forward bend: rest in this standing inversion to bring about a youthful-looking complexion.

Corpse pose: relax for 2 to 3 minutes to gather your energies, but don't drift back to sleep again.

Deep breathing sitting cross-legged: if you want to check your breathing, place your hands on your chest and abdomen, otherwise rest your palms on your thighs.

Full body stretch
(see page 103, step 1)

Corpse pose with legs bent
(see page 20)

Supine twist
(see page 130)

Cat pose
(see page 30)

Child pose
(see page 74)

Mountain pose
(see page 44)

Upstretched hand pose
(see page 82)

Standing wheel pose
(see page 26)

Standing forward bend
(see page 106)

Corpse pose
(see page 98)

Deep breathing sitting cross-legged
(see page 56)

bedtime sequence

Use this routine to help your mind switch off and ease out the stresses that have gathered in your neck and shoulders and around your solar plexus during the day. When you finally get into bed, be reassured that you have sealed the day with your yoga session, and left behind all the tension and preoccupations.

20–30 minutes

Chest expander: gently unlock tension in the neck and shoulders and bring your breathing back into balance.

Head to knee pose: rest the brain in this forward bend as you allow your spine and the back of the legs to give up their tension.

Intense back stretch: relax forward onto cushions if this makes the pose a more effective wind-down.

Thunderbolt pose: feel your sitting bones dropping toward the ground, earthing unwanted energy out of your system. Support yourself with cushions or blocks if this makes relaxation easier.

Torso stretch: let this easy twist bring relief to the spine, then roll onto your back.

Raising knees to chest: massage your spine by rolling from side to side and from shoulders to tailbone.

Bridge pose: this is recommended to alleviate insomnia.

Half shoulderstand: inversions are good at the end of a day to ease out aching shoulders and neck muscles, and still a racing mind. They also take pressure off your legs if you've had a hard day on your feet, helping prevent varicose veins.

Plow pose: for extra relaxation, bend your knees and draw them in against your ears. Relax your arms around the back of your knees. Close your eyes.

Lengthening the out breath in perfect pose: extending the exhalation allows the in breath, when it comes, to be even and full. Work in this anti-insomnia sitting pose

Corpse pose: climb into bed for the final relaxation. This is one of the few times when it's OK to drift off to sleep in Savasana. Alternatively, roll onto your right side, so the left nostril is dominant: breathing through the left nostril calms and relaxes.

Chest expander
(see page 62)

Head to knee pose
(see page 69)

Intense back stretch
(see page 116)

Thunderbolt pose
(see page 96)

Torso stretch
(see page 92)

Raising knees to chest
(see page 21)

Bridge pose
(see page 132)

Half shoulderstand
(see page 135)

Plow pose
(see page 136)

Lengthening the out breath in perfect pose
**(see page 76, steps 1 to 2, then page 97,
steps 3 to 4)**

Corpse pose
(see page 78)

women only sequence

This sequence is safe to follow during your menstrual period, when the poses also ease out cramps and discomfort in the lower back. Practiced over a period of time, these poses can help regulate the menstrual cycle. Remember that you don't have to practice yoga during your period if you don't feel up to it.

30–45 minutes

Hip rotation: warm up the region by rotating the hips, then follow with a figure-of-eight movement.

Corpse pose with legs bent: imagine the abdominal area becoming heavy and sinking toward the floor.

Raising knees to chest: rotate your knees around if it brings relief to the abdomen and lower back.

Supine twist: twists work on the abdominal area, easing the bloating and digestive disorders that can mar this time of the month.

Cobbler pose: this is the woman's pose par excellence, working the organs of the reproductive and urinary systems. After holding, pivot forward from the hips to take your chest and head toward your feet.

Staff pose: stretch up and out of the pelvis to lift heaviness in the abdominal area. Follow on by stretching the legs wide and lengthening up, then forward.

Head to knee pose: forward bends are particularly good during menstruation, and they help relieve abdominal pain and lower-back ache.

Downward facing dog pose: follow this pose by sinking your buttocks back onto your heels, palms planted where they were. Rest for a few moments.

Cobra pose: give your abdomen and pelvis a gentle stretch, but don't come up too far.

Bow pose: take the backward bend a little further, but only if you feel up to it.

Inverted lake pose: this is a safe inversion during menstruation.

Corpse pose: cover yourself with a blanket if you want to coddle yourself.

Hip rotation
(see page 42)

Corpse pose with legs bent
(see page 20)

Raising knees to chest
(see page 21)

Supine twist
(see page 130)

Cobbler pose
(see page 32)

Staff pose
(see page 68)

Head to knee pose
(see page 69)

Downward facing dog pose
(see page 64)

Cobra pose
(see page 112)

Bow pose
(see page 114)

Inverted lake pose
(see page 34)

Corpse pose
(see page 36)

energizing sequence

When your mind can no longer focus, your body won't do what you ask it to, and you feel irritable and fed up, you need a yoga energy fix. Let this sequence refresh your brain, restore your motivation, and enliven fatigued muscles.

30–45 minutes

Throat and chest stretch: use the throat and chest stretch and the leg and neck raises from this sequence to stimulate your circulation and get your innate energy flowing.

Warrior pose sequence: for stamina and power, realign your body in Mountain Pose, then use the Warrior postures to stretch the spine strongly and make expansive movements with the arms and legs. From Warrior II, take your left hand down beside your left foot and stretch your right arm upward. Look up. Hold for 10 to 30 seconds. Keeping your legs in position, turn your torso square over your front knee and stretch your arms forward, palms together. Raise your arms into Warrior I. Repeat to the other side.

Standing forward bend: rest here, bathing the brain in rejuvenating blood, until you have caught your breath.

Dog pose sequence: hold Downward Facing Dog for 30 seconds, then bend your elbows and look forward. Keeping your hips high, take your forehead, then your chin toward the floor and push on your palms to bring your chest forward and up into Upward Facing Dog. Hold briefly, then press your hips up and back into Downward Dog. Switch between the two poses for a minute or so.

Child pose: sink your hips back and rest here until your breathing is steady again.

Thunderbolt pose: tuck your toes under and sit back on your heels, holding as long as possible to enliven the toes and soles.

Lateral sitting twist: this twist is thought to ignite your dormant internal energy.

Camel pose: open your chest fully to allow your breathing to become more effective, bringing as much fresh oxygen as possible into your system with the inhalations, and permitting maximum carbon dioxide to be expelled with the exhalations.

Shoulderstand: this suffuses the brain and upper body, including vital glands, with a good flow of oxygenated blood, bringing you back to life. It also boosts the heart and lungs, and gets the lymphatic system flowing to drain the body of waste matter.

Fish pose: perform after Shoulderstand.

Skull shining: continue the cleansing with this totally invigorating breath technique.

Corpse pose: use the energizing light visualization.

Throat and chest stretch
(see page 104)

Warrior pose sequence
(see page 50 & 52)

Standing forward bend
(see page 106)

Dog pose sequence
(see pages 64–67)

Child pose
(see page 74)

Thunderbolt pose
(see page 96)

Lateral sitting twist
(see page 94)

Camel pose
(see page 72)

Shoulderstand
(see page 134)

Fish pose
(see page 138)

Skull shining
(see page 140)

Corpse pose
(see page 120)

relaxing sequence

This routine calms the nervous system and rests the body by relieving mental tension and an overactive mind, and by easing out areas of tightness that have built up over a busy day.

30–45 minutes

Mountain pose: realign your body and locate your center before you start to diffuse tension.

Extended triangle pose: this easy standing pose expands your chest to allow you to breathe more easily. Work with a block if it helps you relax.

Extended side angle stretch: extends the sides of the body, often neglected in everyday movements.

Downward facing dog: start to wind down now as this pose slows the heartbeat while stretching out tense neck and shoulders, and easing tension headaches.

Standing forward bend: let it all go, feeling relief from stiffness in the lower back and the backs of the legs releasing.

Child pose: rest here until you feel calm.

Torso stretch: unwind your spine with a gentle twist.

Upright extended foot pose: leg raises enable your lower back to rest, firmly supported by the floor.

Shoulderstand: the ultimate wind-down. Close your eyes, if desired.

Fish pose: broaden your chest to prepare for deep, relaxing breathing.

Corpse pose: relinquish control of your body and mind.

Alternate nostril breathing in half lotus pose: complete your breathing practice by working with the calming left nostril only as you sit in one of the traditional poses for meditation.

Mountain pose
(see page 44)

Extended triangle pose
(see page 48)

Extended side angle stretch
(see page 88)

Downward facing dog pose
(see page 64)

Standing forward bend
(see page 106)

Child pose
(see page 74)

Torso stretch
(see page 92)

Upright extended foot pose
(see page 128)

Shoulderstand
(see page 134)

Fish pose
(see page 138)

Corpse pose
(see page 58)

Alternate nostril breathing in
half lotus pose
(see page 118)

yoga at your desk

It's sensible to take a proper break from your work every hour or so when you sit hunched over a desk or at a computer. Grab a drink of water, then use these exercises to open up the chest, stretch out the hands and wrists, and revive crunched up neck and shoulders. This sequence will keep your brain alert and body relaxed, enhancing your productivity and ability to make decisions.

5 minutes

sitting sequence

pose	method
Chest expander for the upper body **see page 62**	Move your chair back from the desk, then sit on the front of the seat to follow the Chest Expander exercise from a sitting position to stretch the wrists and elbow joints, free the chest, and take blood to the brain.
Upstretched hand pose **see page 82**	Again work from sitting, extending your spine well before bending left and right.
Standing twist **see page 28**	Still sitting, perform this movement with the upper body without crossing the legs.
Deep breathing **see page 56**	Still sitting and without crossing the legs, use this simple technique to remind yourself to breathe from the abdomen.

standing sequence

pose	method
Half forward bend **see page 24**	Bend forward to your desk, or to the photocopier to re-energize the back and legs, and free mental tension.
Standing forward bend **see page 106**	This sends blood to your brain and upper body, which is recuperative when you have been sitting upright for some time, and promotes alertness. Work with arms loosely folded above your head at first. As an alternative, lift your head, straighten your arms, and look forward.
Tree pose **see page 46**	Balance postures focus concentration while awakening the spine. Practice inconspicuously by taking the raised foot to your opposite ankle, still keeping the hips opening outward. Or invite colleagues to join you!

yoga in the car

Welcome traffic gridlock as an opportunity to achieve some yoga practice. When you're sitting in a jam or stuck at lights, try some of these ideas to ward off frustration, revive tired, tense muscles, and keep the blood circulating. Hold each position for a few breath cycles. Don't get so involved that you lose your awareness of car safety, however.

5–10 minutes

pose	method
Neck roll and shoulder shrug **see page 40**	After completing these energizers, gently exercise your eyes. Keeping your head and neck still and facing front, look up with your eyes only, then down. Hold each gaze for a few seconds, resisting the urge to blink. Then look left, and right, followed by left up and right down; right up and left down. Finally, keeping your head still, circle your eyes around an imaginary clockface.
Staff pose **see page 68**	Try this modified pose: sitting as you are, press on your palms to lengthen your spine and open your wrists, palms, and elbows.
Standing wheel pose **see page 26**	Shift your buttocks forward onto the front of the seat and use the upper body movements only from this position; don't take your arms overhead.
Knee and ankle circle **see page 43**	From sitting, focus on the knee and ankle exercises: energizing static feet and legs keeps blood circulating to your extremities.
Victory breath in perfect pose **see page 76**	When you arrive at your destination, sit quietly and focus your breathing with this technique for a few minutes, then stretch out with the simple warm up on pages 38–41.

index